from the COVER

15 Memorable Projects for Quilt Lovers

Mary Leman Austin

& *Quilter's Newsletter Magazine* Editors & Contributors

C&T PUBLISHING

Text © 2004 Mary Leman Austin

Artwork © 2004 Primedia
Special Interest Publications
and C&T Publishing

Publisher
Amy Marson

Editorial Director
Gailen Runge

Editor
Lynn Koolish

Technical Editors
*Diane Kennedy-Jackson/
Terry Stroin*

Copyeditor/Proofreader
*Linda Dease Smith/
Stacy Chamness*

Book Designer
Nancy Biltcliff

Design Directors
Diane Pedersen, Dave Nash

Cover Designer
Kristy Konitzer

Production Assistant
Luke Mulks

Quilt Photography
*Mellisa Karlin Mahoney,
unless otherwise noted*

Published by
*C&T Publishing, Inc., P.O. Box
1456, Lafayette, California, 94549*

Front cover
Fire Lily *by Barbara Williams*

Back cover
Working Out the Blues
by Ruth Hans

Library of Congress Cataloging-in-Publication Data

Austin, Mary Leman.
  From the cover : 15 memorable projects for quilt lovers / Mary Leman Austin & Quilter's newsletter magazine editors & contributors.
      p. cm.
  Includes bibliographical references and index.
  ISBN 1-57120-246-3 (paper trade)
  1. Patchwork--Patterns. 2. Quilting. 3. Patchwork quilts. I. Quilter's newsletter magazine. II. Title.
  TT835.A94437 2004
  746.46'041--dc22

                                                         2004001908

Printed in China
10 9 8 7 6 5 4 3 2 1

Table of Contents

Acknowledgments

Thanks to our many contributors and loyal subscribers. A special thanks to all the co-workers and colleagues who helped create Quilter's Newsletter Magazine *throughout the years. Any omittances are unintentional.*

THE FAMILY TEAM

Bonnie Leman	Mary Leman	David Leman
George Leman	Emilie Leman	Andrew Leman
Megan Leman	Georgianne Leman	Matthew Leman

QUILTER'S NEWSLETTER MAGAZINE EDITORIAL STAFF

Jennifer L. Acerbi	Susan Geddes	Caroline Reardon
Deidre C. Adams	Allison Gray	Vivian Ritter
George Becker	Lee Greengross	Joyce A. Robinson
Madalene Becker	Roy L. Hale	Annie Tregay Segal
Debbe Benson	N. Kay Jesse	Marie Shirer
Irene Berry	Pamela Kittrell	Barbara Smith
Cindy Brick	Michelle Kucharski	Janet Jo Smith
Ellie Brown	Chris Lawrence	Jeannie M. Spears
Penny Conyers	Lauri Linch-Zadel	Marla Gibbs Stefanelli
Carol Crowley	Linda Lynch	Belinda Sturgis
Lou Cunningham	Jan Magee	Karen Gillis Taylor
Jerry DeFelice	Mellisa Karlin Mahoney	Louise O. Townsend
Kathy DuBois	Judy Martin	Lois Marilyn Verma
Theresa Eisinger	Linda Martin	Sandee Wachal
Susan Ennis	Pat McClure-Madorin	Hari Walner
Sara Felton	Laurie Meador	Kathryn Wagar Wright
Sue Ficca	Clara Murray	Su Wright
	Donna Nelson	
	Karen O'Dowd	

COLUMNISTS AND CONTRIBUTING EDITORS

Norma Bradley Allen
Alex Anderson
Virginia Avery
Marcella Bechtel
Cuesta Benberry
Jinny Beyer
Barbara Brackman

Jean Dubois
Theo Eson
Robbie Fanning
Myrna Geisbrecht
Jeffrey Gutcheon
Betsey Harris
Dixie Haywood
Jonathan Holstein
Carter Houck

Michael James
Helen Kelley
Jean Ray Laury
Bonnie Leonard
Mary Coyne Penders
Victoria Stuart
Deb Wagner

OTHER STAFF

Mardee Arabalo
Scott Ashley
Pat Bachman
Tina Battock
Ron Beeson
David Bender
Judy Benjamin
Michelle Blumenschein
Cara Bock
Doris Boisvert
Terry Boyer
Julia Breidenstein
Rhonda Brennan
Elaine Bruggeman
Robin Burrell
Bobby Butler
Wade Clark
Darcy Cruwys

Frances Dellarosa
Betty Dufficy
Kim Edwards
Suzan Ellis
Ray Ellison
Debbie Everett
Berniece Fair
Mildred Ferris
Mike Fitzpatrick
Jane Flynn
Tina Fugate
Mary Gibbs
Joyce Gonzalez
Sara Gunn
Laurie Halvorsen
Cammie Hamilton
Lisa Harris

Nadene M. Hartley
Marcia Hatcher
Lynn Hochschild
Colleen Hodnik
Bill Howell
Jan Howitt
Kelly Howitt-Chestnut
Christopher Howley
Laurel Johnson
Ray Jones
Michael Kappus
Bob Kaslik
Becky Land
Al LeBois
Betsy Loeff
Margie Mahoney
Ivy Malden
Toni Martin

Mary Martinez
Michelle May
Loretta McKercher
Magalie McLemore
Heather McNair
Alice Mealman
Stephanie Michas
Mollie Miller
Gwen Mumbrue
Clara Murray
Janice Murray
Alissa Norton
Susan O'Brien
Lisa O'Bryan
David O'Neil
Jo Page
Elizabeth Phillips

Sylvia Probst
Dana Raven
Diane Richardson
John Rusin
Nancy Scanland
Carlyn Scarpino
Mary Schmidt
Pat Schmitz
Angela Skalla
Joanne Skeen
Rose St. Louis
Susan Hazel Tyler
Beverly Vigil
Diane Wenzel
Amanda Woodson
Marie Woodson
R. S. Wotkyns III
Jane Younger

Special thanks to Irene Berry, Penny Conyers, Jan Magee, Vivian Ritter, and Janet Jo Smith for their assistance with this project.

kitchen table *Story*

The cover of the first-ever *Quilter's Newsletter Magazine* was labeled "Introductory Sample Issue" and showed a quilted pillow bearing the Moon Flowers appliqué design. This cover was an invitation to read at your leisure about quilting and to participate in a more active way by ordering the pattern for the cover project and the other patterns and tools advertised inside. The appliqué shown was stitched by machine with a zigzag satin stitch.

1968 In 1968, my parents George and Bonnie Leman were both schoolteachers in Denver, Colorado, working two jobs each to support a growing family of six children. Always seeking opportunities for additional income, they discussed starting a mail-order business that Mom could run at the kitchen table with Dad's help on the weekends. Mom, ever a devotee of the public library, began to research product ideas.

In the 1960s, active quiltmakers had few resources and limited opportunity for contact with each other. Quilt literature was hard to locate, often out-of-print, and most of those who made quilts traded or copied the old patterns. Several small quilt-pattern pamphlets appeared in the 1960s, most notably *Aunt Kate's Quilting Bee* (1962–1966), published by Glenna Boyd, and *Nimble Needle Treasures*, published intermittently from 1962–1980 by Pat Almy.

There were no quilt shops, and available fabrics were mostly synthetics. Quilt contests might be found at county or state fairs. In 1967, San Francisco chapters of the Dorcas Society (a nationwide organization that raised funds to feed and clothe the poor) priced hand quilting at $67 for a king-size quilt, including marking, Dacron batting, backing, and binding. This fee was a considerable increase from the previous century, when Dorcas chapters charged approximately $2 (1¢ per hour) for a hand-quilted king-size quilt.

Mom, experienced in sewing and needlecraft as well as writing, was the owner of a treasured scrapbook of her mother's collection of *Kansas City Star* patterns. She found the subject of quilts particularly interesting, and as she researched them, she fell in love with

a quilter's TIMELINE

1960s

✳ The Kutztown Pennsylvania Dutch Festival, established in 1950, continues its quilt contest and auction tradition. ✳ **The Freedom Bee is founded in Alabama in 1966, and sells handmade quilts to**

their designs and history. Seeing a need for more patterns for quilters of the day, she thought if patterns were good, templates might be even better. Mom started tracing and re-drafting some of the classic designs; Dad located a source of lightweight plastic that he could cut into square and triangle shapes on a paper cutter.

An investment of $5 was made for a one-time classified ad in a mid-western weekly newspaper. I will always remember the day that Mom came running out of the house into the backyard waving the first order for $13 worth of templates and patterns, as excited as if she had held a winning lottery ticket. This order and others paid for the ad and the template supplies, with enough left over to buy a few more ads. Leman Publications/Quilts & Other Comforts was off and running, and my parents were in the quilt pattern business.

Before too long, a customer comment inspired Mom's idea of a newsletter for quiltmakers. Inexperienced in publishing, but still knowing the way to the library, she once again began to do research, but did not find as much information as she had hoped. However, she was determined to make her "Quilter's Newsletter" as professional looking as she could. "We started on a shoestring," she has said, "and all I had to work with was a $25 used portable Royal typewriter, and a vast ignorance of procedures for preparing material for printing. The printer rejected the first sample I showed him, explaining that it was not dark enough to reproduce successfully.

So, for the first few issues, before I took each page out of the typewriter, I carefully and slowly re-rolled it back to the beginning and typed it a second time to darken each letter. If I made a typo, I had to start over. If correction fluid had yet been invented, I hadn't heard of it."

I remember Mom creating the little quilt that made up *Quilter's Newsletter Magazine's* first logo—she carefully traced and cut out the letter shapes from a quilted piece of pre-printed-patchwork fabric. QNM's first cover subject, the Moon Flowers pillow, was designed and made by Mom, and the pattern was offered for sale in that issue.

1969 Mom and Dad's seventh child, Matthew (welcomed by his siblings, Megan, Mary, Emilie, Georgianne, David, and Andrew), was born on the same day that the first issue of QNM came back from the printer. Dad brought a copy to the hospital, and Mom has often recollected that the "scent of the ink and paper was every bit as sweet as the fragrance of roses."

In the third issue, Mom pledged to her readers to honor the following New Year's resolutions, "I resolve to do my best to make QNM the best magazine there is or ever was for quilters. I resolve to have something for new quilters as well as experienced quilters in every issue. I resolve to have new ideas or patterns as well as old traditional patterns in

Mom and Dad themselves produced the work of art on this cover, but it wasn't a quilt. It was their four-month-old baby Matthew, who shared a birthday with QNM. This has been the only QNM cover photo that doesn't have a single quilt in it. Mom wrote in the issue about what she had planned for future covers, and included a plea for quilt-makers and quilt owners to preserve their quilts with a photographic record, both for posterity and to share with QNM.

stylish stores in New York City, with proceeds going to the cooperative of impoverished women who make the quilts. In 1968 the Mountain Artisans Co-op of West Virginia is founded to create jobs for quiltmakers in the Appalachian region, marketing their handmade

quilts to upscale customers. ✳ A handful of quilting books becomes available, including Ruby McKim's *101 Patchwork Patterns*, Donna Renshaw's *Quilting, a Revived Art*, and Jean Ray Laury's *Appliqué Stitchery*.

QUILTER'S NEWSLETTER

Nos. 9 & 10   The Magazine for Quilt Lovers   1970

Flower Basket Petit Point Quilt

Flower Basket Petit Point, 94" × 92", by Grace McCance Snyder, 1942–1943. With permission, Grace based her pattern on a plate originally designed by German artist Wendelin Grossman and manufactured by Salem China Company in Salem, Ohio. The patches are so tiny (eight triangles sewn together are the size of a postage stamp) that the large quilt resembles a needle-point. This accomplished quilter from Nebraska and her quilts are legendary, but this quilt is her most famous of all.

Quilt photo courtesy of Caxton Printers, Ltd.

every issue. I resolve that I will consider your ideas and suggestions, and that I will include as many of them as possible in the magazine."

1970 In 1970, Mom made a valuable connection to an exceptional resource, the notable quilt collection of the Denver Art Museum, at that time curated by Imelda De-Graw. Though the magazine's black-and-white format didn't do justice to the quilts, two of the collection's masterpieces, Grace Snyder's *Flower Basket Petit Point* and Charlotte Jane Whitehill's *Flower Basket*, graced the covers of *QNM* in 1970.

Throughout the early '70s, Mom fine-tuned *QNM*'s voice and content. There was always a block contest going on, and the magazine presented many original reader designs. She offered classic patterns as well as any quilt-making technique that she could devise or had heard about. The News section usually contained information from newspaper clippings sent in by readers from all around the country. She continued to develop resources for photographs of fine antique quilts, and experimented with all sorts of ideas for articles.

Throughout the early '70s, Mom fine-tuned *QNM*'s voice and content.

In the eighth issue she promised to leave out the recipes she'd been including as "Mother's Kitchen Diary" and reader recipe exchange, although not before publishing the following:

"How to Preserve Children . . .

Take one large grassy field, a half-dozen small children, 3 small dogs, 1 narrow strip of brook—pebbly if possible; mix the children with the dogs and empty them into the field, stirring continually. . . . Sprinkle the field with flowers; pour brook gently over pebbles; cover all with a deep blue sky and bake in the sun. When children are well browned they may be removed. Will be found right and ready for setting away to cool in the bathtub."

I have recently seen the above recipe on the Internet, but in 1970 Mom found it credited to Mrs. J. T. Able in the 1915 *Linneus Cookbook* (Linneus was the closest "big" town to Mom's hometown of Purdin, Missouri).

These days we'd include sunscreen and insect repellent in the recipe, but Mom's friendly, family-oriented writing style was a key ingredient in the strong rapport that she built with her readers. They became her partners in the enterprise through their regular correspondence, suggestions, and participation.

Some features from those early issues continue today including the "Meetin' Place," "What's New in Quilting," "Book Reviews,"

1970
✳ VISTA volunteers help organize the Red Cloud-Wakpamni Quilting Association to sell quilts made by Oglala Sioux of the South Dakota Pine Ridge Reservation. ✳ *Glamour* magazine publishes a fashion spread on patchwork clothing, including a figure-flattering skirt made of yo-yos priced at $80. ✳ Seven women in the Washington, D.C., area found the National Quilting Association.

✳ Van Nostrand Reinhold Company publishes Jean Ray Laury's *Quilts and Coverlets: A Contemporary Approach*.

1971
✳ "Abstract Design in American Quilts" is exhibited at the Whitney Museum of American Art in New York City. Sixty works from the Holstein/van der Hoof quilt collection show the link between modern abstract art and bed quilts of the

series patterns, "Easy Lessons," and "Quilting Bee." And of course patterns, both old-time traditional ones and contemporary originals, designed by readers or Mom.

"Grandma's Corner" was one of the magazine's most popular columns. Originally written in issues #3–#8 by Mrs. Garnett Leonard, the column was taken over by Theo Eson in issue #9. Theo's writing appeared regularly until 1979, and her column won twelve journalism awards, including top honors from the National Federation of Press Women. (In 1979, she officially retired and took a tramp steamer journey around South America.)

All of us kids pitched in at the family company. My sisters and I helped with filing, order-filling, and label-sticking; I did the art (I use the term loosely) for the magazine; and our little brothers mainly entertained us and acted as child models for many patchwork toys and garments. Mom's brother, Roy Hale, shot much of the photography for the magazine for more than fifteen years. He photographed numerous quilts in museum collections that had never previously been professionally shot, and he captured images of many significant contemporary works. Dad continued teaching, but spent every spare moment on the growth of our family business. My folks put in many long nights.

1971

By 1971, the workload had become too much for the family to handle, so Mom hired first one, then another high-school student to help part-time. More space was needed as well, so Mom and Dad decided to construct a small addition to our house. Permits were required for this, and on the day the building inspector came to view the plans, he found two people typing labels in our basement, and decided something nefarious was going on. Mom and Dad received a notice to move the business out of our home within a week or be shut down, so Dad found a tiny office right away. It was a mixed blessing—Mom missed being able to work at home, but the business expanded more quickly than it might have otherwise.

One of QNM's best cover stories that year was about one of America's finest quiltmakers, Bertha Stenge, whose daughter had decided to offer some of her mother's quilts for sale. The black-and-white format didn't do justice to the photographs of Mrs. Stenge's exquisite work, but she was quoted as saying that "the two things you need most in making appliqué quilts are plenty of patience and a warm iron." (See page 18 for one of Bertha Stenge's quilts.)

1972

The diversity that has been QNM's hallmark was established from the beginning. A sampling of the articles published in 1972 includes how-to features on making bias-tape quilts, plenty of classic patterns, new designs from the readers, quilt puzzles and poems, an article about notable collectors Joel and Kate Kopp and their New York shop

Indian Paint Brush, 90" × 90", by Charlotte Jane Whitehill, 1934. The photo shows one of nine blocks, modeled on an heirloom quilt. Charlotte was part of a distinguished group of Kansas quiltmakers of the 1920s and 1930s. Charlotte's quilts are in the permanent collection of the Denver Art Museum.

Bride's Album Quilt, 98" × 97", various makers in Baltimore, 1848–1849. This block exemplifies quilts in the Baltimore Museum of Art collection. The name of George Holtzman is signed in the center block, along with a heart-and-wheel design, indicating the quilt was likely made for George's fiancée.

nineteenth century. The exhibit gets rave reviews, and the quilts go on to be shown worldwide. The collection is instrumental in the growing revival of quilting. ✹ **Fairfield Processing introduces the first needle-punched polyester batting.** ✹ Hearthside Press published Mom's book *Quick and Easy Quilting*, the first book to cover the quilt-as-you-go technique.

1972

✹ In Mill Valley, California, the exhibit "A Patch In Time" draws large crowds. The aim of the show is to illustrate the continually evolving art of quiltmaking, and the sponsors hang such diverse works as antique Log Cabins and crazy quilts side by side with contemporary pictorial appliqué and tie-dyed quilts. ✹ For the first time, the Kansas University Museum of Art exhibits its extensive collection of antique quilts, a collection estimated by some as second only to that held by the Smithsonian.

Crazy Quilt, 70" × 82", by Mrs. Edward Harmon, around 1860. Made in Ireland, the quilt contains a variety of fabrics not usually found in quilts, including Victorian lace house curtains and a fur-like fabric as the grass in front of the house. The quilt has extensive detailed embroidery throughout.

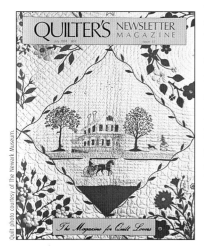

The Emeline Dean Quilt (detail), 92" × 92", by Emeline Dean, around 1860. From the Newark Museum collection in New Jersey. In this center block of the album quilt, the maker depicted herself as a child with her horse and cart, dog, and home. It's believed the album quilt was completed for Emeline's wedding.

America Hurrah, a photo and story about a quilt made by president Calvin Coolidge at the age of ten, and pictures of quilts made for Presidents Johnson and Nixon.

QNM listed several new summer quilt shows, half of which were exhibits presented by non-profit quilting cooperatives such as the Freedom Bee and Coty-award winning Mountain Artisans.

One of the first display advertisements to appear in QNM was for the Howard Johnson's Motor Lodge in Mill Valley, California, which offered special quilter's rates to visitors coming in to see the second "A Patch in Time" exhibit.

Dad finally left his teaching position to devote all his energies to the magazine and mail-order business. One day Mom said, quite casually I am sure, that it would be interesting to have a small shop in which to display all the merchandise we offered by mail order. Before she had a chance to consider this remark or take it back, Dad, a man of action, went out and rented an empty grocery store, and the family began to prepare for another office move.

1973 Mom and Dad opened the Quilts & Other Comforts shop, and invited readers to visit. They offered fabric, all manner of quiltmaking supplies (a limited range at that time), new and vintage quilts for sale, classes, books, and patterns.

The fuel crisis of the early 1970s had some unexpected ramifications—as polyester blends became more expensive to produce, they began to fall out of favor with quiltmakers. Fortunately, cotton fabric became more affordable and more widely available than it had been for years. Paper prices increased by 50 percent, with no guarantee of availability, and it was a guessing game from month to month whether our printer would have enough paper for the press run, up to about 10,000 copies by then. The size of QNM increased from sixteen to thirty-two black-and-white pages so paper was indeed a concern.

Mom mentioned in a 1973 editorial that machine quilting could be as beautiful as hand quilting, and was a practical way to finish quilts quickly. Although QNM's content was primarily focused on traditional quilt patterns and techniques, the magazine published photos of art quilts by Sonya Lee Barrington and University of Colorado professor Richard Dudley.

1974 In 1974, QNM began two-color printing on glossy paper. This was an interesting time for all of us, as we learned how to prepare the pages for this sophisticated format. The manual typewriter was long gone by then, and Mom now used an IBM Selectric. I had new art tools: press-on letters, graphic tape, a rapidograph pen, and amberlith. (If you have no idea what these items are, don't worry, as they are now completely obsolete methods of

1973

✳ *Prevention* magazine reports that occupational therapists and research studies agree that those who participate in quiltmaking and other needlework activities live longer and enjoy life more. ✳ Quiltmaking is regularly mentioned in almost all mainstream women's magazines as patchwork and quilted wearables and bed quilts continue to gain popularity. ✳ *Ladies Circle Patchwork Quilts* publishes its first issue, and Marti Michell founds Yours Truly, Inc.

1974

✳ The number of significant quilt exhibitions continues to grow, with the Metropolitan Museum of Art in New York and the Denver Art Museum among them. ✳ Some significant books on quiltmaking are published, including Jonathan Holstein's *The Pieced Quilt* and Beth Gutcheon's highly influential *Perfect Patchwork Primer*, which encourages contemporary quiltmakers to experiment with original design solutions using traditional patchwork elements.

With the arrival of the bicentennial in 1976, quiltmaking grew even more popular.

Stars and Stripes, 78" × 84", maker unknown, between 1840 and 1860, an original design based on the Variable Star pattern. After being "collected" in Michigan, it became part of the inventory of Mary Strickler's Quilt, a shop specializing in antique quilts in San Rafael, California.

preparing art for printing.) Mailing labels were still typed with carbons for copies and applied by hand, and Dad loaded the addressed magazines in our van and took them to our local post office.

Jinny Beyer, well-known to quilters worldwide as a lecturer, teacher, judge, author, and maker of fine quilts won QNM's "Mariner's Compass block" contest.

1975
Artist and quiltmaker Susan Ennis joined our team of the family, editorial assistant Lou Cunningham, and three part-time customer service specialists. The magazine's first full-color pages were printed in the July 1975 issue. Dad dealt with the printers, but found the experience frustrating and expensive. Since he always enjoyed a challenge and had a do-it-yourself philosophy, he decided we could print the magazine ourselves. So, he purchased printing and bindery equipment, set up in a warehouse near the Quilts & Other Comforts shop, and Dad and I, along with a couple of fellows with printing experience, began to produce the magazine. We made the printing plates, printed the

pages, folded and stapled them together, and trimmed them on a huge paper cutter to make the finished magazines.

Dad dealt with most of the day-to-day details of running the mail-order business that was growing by leaps and bounds, just like the magazine. In 1975, the Quilts & Other Comforts catalog was thirty-two pages packed with newly available books, kits, and lots of patterns designed and developed by Mom and the staff.

1976
With the arrival of the bicentennial in 1976, quiltmaking grew even more popular. Many works created for the bicentennial were forerunners in a new trend toward large-scale pictorial quilts, designed to be displayed on the wall rather than a bed. Mom coined the term "wall quilt" for this new style of quilt.

QNM featured its first truly contemporary cover subject in the May 1976 issue, a silk-screened quilt by Jeannie Spears (who was later to become a senior editor at QNM). The magazine retained a focus on traditional quiltmaking, but also presented contemporary work

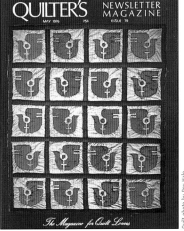

Red, White, and Woman, 80" × 100", by Jeannie M. Spears, 1976. This quilt was made in honor of the bicentennial and International Women's Year. Jeannie batiked the design for the blocks onto muslin, and stuffed the trapunto after quilting each block separately with the quilt-as-you-go method.

1975
✴ Bicentennial fever kicks in and bicentennial quilt and block contests are everywhere, sponsored by Fairfield Processing, Stearns and Foster, the National Grange, and QNM among others. Popular contemporary quilt styles of the day include medallion quilts and blue-jean quilts. ✴ The Holstein/van der Hoof collection is shown in Tokyo, and a year later Sandi Fox brings her exhibit "America in Patchwork" to Japan. Both events plant the seeds of a quilting craze that explodes in that country.

1976
✴ A quilt and pillow pattern by Betty Boyink is licensed as an official bicentennial commemorative, and she is invited to the White House to present the original quilt. ✴ Karey Bresenhan organizes Quilt Fair '76, sponsored by the Quilt Guild of Greater Houston; the event is the forerunner to today's International Quilt Market and Festival. ✴ Many bicentennial quilt exhibitions and contests take place. "Quilts in Women's Lives," organized by Pat Ferrero, Linda Reuther, and Julie Silber at the San Francisco Art Institute, turns out to be the most widely attended exhibit in the Institute's history.

Blazing Stars, 65" × 75", and *Double Wedding Ring*, 72" × 72", makers unknown, made around 1930. The quilts were part of the collection of Quilts & Other Comforts, the quilt shop and mail order company based in Wheat Ridge, Colorado, that was the sister establishment of *QNM*.

Ray of Light, 80" × 91", by Jinny Beyer, 1977. This handmade masterpiece won grand prize in the "1978 Great American Quilt Contest", beating out more than 10,000 other entries. The quilt is one of the most widely recognized quilt images.

and new methods of modern quilt making including techniques for leather, as well as batiked, tie-dyed, Native American, and silk-screened quilts.

QNM's Quiltmobile began to travel the country. Dad drove and took one of us kids along to help out on each trip. As these trips held the possibility of staying at a motel with a swimming pool, they were considered a plum assignment. The Quiltmobile visited California, Nevada, Missouri, Arizona, Kansas, Utah, Washington, and Oregon.

The Quilts & Other Comforts shop hosted the first American exhibit of British quilts, curated and organized by Jenny Shinn with Hazel Carter.

In its general instructions *QNM* still recommended the use of traditional templates without seam allowances as the best method for accurate patchwork, but published some of Barbara Johannah's innovative strip-piecing techniques. Johannah's book, *Quick Quilting—Make a Quilt This Weekend*, promoted her at-that-time revolutionary idea of making a quilt from new yardage off the bolt, using assembly-line methods for cutting, marking, strip piecing, and making triangle units.

1977 The divide between contemporary quilters and traditional quilters grew wider with the results of the *Indianapolis Star* "Flower Garden Quilt" contest. Entries were required to incorporate twenty-five of the Flower Garden block patterns by Ruby McKim, and the rules stated that entries would be judged on innovative use of the old patterns to achieve a contemporary, personal quilt. The winning quilt was created using reverse appliqué and bright vivid colors on bright and dark backgrounds. Of the 6,000 viewers of the quilts, nearly 1,500 wrote comments for the suggestion box. The majority were critical of the judges' decision.

QNM published Mom's "Standards for Judging Quilts in Competition," a scoring methodology for quilt show organizers and judges.

Barbara Brackman contributed her first article on how to organize a quilt collection to the June 1977 issue, marking the beginning of a long association with *QNM*.

1978 Mom and Dad decided to get out of the day-to-day work of running our quilt shop in order to concentrate on the publications and catalogs, and soon the shop

QNM published Mom's "Standards for Judging Quilts in Competition," a scoring methodology for quilt show organizers and judges.

1977

 In Warrenton, Michigan, 20,000 visitors attend the National Bicentennial Quilt Exposition and Contest. ☀ The Santa Clara Valley Quilt Association establishes the first-ever quilt museum in San Jose, California.

1978

☀ The U.S. Postal Service issues a thirteen-cent Commemorative Basket Stamp, and it eventually graces more than

275,000,000 letters. ☀ Several national conferences for quilters take place: The Southern Quilt Symposium in Tennessee, the First Continental Quilt Congress in Virginia, the Kansas Quilt Symposium in Kansas, and the West Coast Quilting Conference in Oregon all draw eager visitors.

1979

☀ Nancy Crow conceives and organizes "Quilt National," the first juried show dedicated to celebrating the

manager, Berniece Fair, took over the ownership of the Quilts & Other Comforts store.

It was an exciting time at *QNM* as we moved the magazine operations into a new building. We loved the new space that felt so luxuriously large at the time. Mom and Dad each had their own office, with Mom's looking out into the *QNM* editorial workspace and Dad's having a view of the mail-order area. The magazine's readership had increased to a point that our in-house printers could no longer manage the volume, so we decided to buy outside printing services for the magazine. We worked with several different printing companies over the next few years, a saga on its own. Dad negotiated with the printers initially, but Mom and I were the primary contacts for the actual work. We encountered a bit of patronizing attitude, based in part, we suspected, on our gender and in part on our subject matter. Mostly, we met and worked with many kind and talented people who shared their knowledge and helped us make the magazine more professional looking, issue by issue.

1979 Louise O. Townsend, a very skilled quiltmaker and talented writer, joined the staff of *QNM*. Louise had a great impact on *QNM*, and her passion for organization and accuracy was an invaluable contribution to the magazine over the years.

An ad in *QNM* offered kits for "a chic, smocked gingham hat and matching gathered jabot, just right for pantsuits and a perfect choice for bridesmaids hats." This was not our product idea, but we did manufacture Patt-o-graph (fifteen different kinds of graph paper for drafting and designing quilts); Plastigraph (grid-printed template plastic); Stick-o-yard (a yardstick printed on adhesive backed paper, for sticking to your cutting table); Patch-a-pooch (a kit for a patchwork dog jacket); the Quilt-as-You-Go frame; precut Lone Star kits; and many, many patterns.

QNM ran a series of articles called "Getting Down to Business: Quilters as Professionals," on the topic of how to successfully make a career as a quiltmaker, a choice unheard of ten years previously.

Copyright law had developed into an issue for quiltmakers, with as many questions and confusions as we still seem to experience today.

Four quilts from the first Quilt National juried show for art quilts appeared together on one *QNM* cover.

From an initial print run in 1969 of 5,000 copies and no certainty about a second issue, *QNM* subscribers now exceeded 100,000.

1980 In 1980, Judy Martin brought her quiltmaking, design, and writing talents to *QNM*. Judy was without peer in machine piecing techniques, and her prodigious creative output was instrumental in *QNM*'s growth in

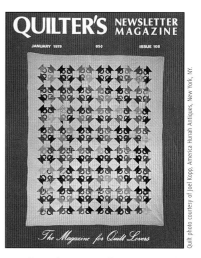

Basket Quilt, aproximately 60" × 72", maker unknown, 1875. The repetition of the simple basket design appealed to the stamp selection committee for the U. S. Postal Service. The quilt was a model for an American Folk Art stamp released in 1978.

Iris Quilt, 76" × 89", by Hannah Haynes Headlee, made in the 1930s. Hannah dyed one of the ten purple fabrics to get the perfect shade, a practice unheard of in her day. She may have been inspired to make a floral quilt by her friend Rose Kretsinger, but all of Hannah's quilts were original designs. This photo was a winner in *QNM*'s cover photo contest.

contemporary quilt artist. It is held at the Dairy Barn in Athens, Ohio, and 390 quilt entries are received from 196 artists. ✸ **Barbara Brackman publishes the first volume of her eight-volume *Encyclopedia of Pieced Patterns*.** ✸ *Lap Quilting with Georgia Bonesteel*, the first quilting-themed TV show, premiers on public television. By 2004, the show will air on more than 160 PBS stations nationwide. ✸ **The Continental Quilting Congress establishes the Quilters Hall of Fame.**

1980

✸ Priscilla Miller of Concord Fabrics and Donna Wilder of Fairfield Processing Corp. conceive and organize the first quilted wearables challenge and exhibit, the Fairfield Fashion Show. ✸ **Marti Michell of Yours Truly, Inc. and Mary Ellen Hopkins, introduce rotary cutters to the U.S. quiltmaking market, paving the way for contemporary quiltmaking techniques.** ✸ In California the American Quilt Study Group meets for the first time.

This cover, a departure from the typical *QNM* cover, features Jerome DeFelice. Quilts (clockwise from top left): *Italian Rose*, 42" × 45"; *Geese in the Pond*, 44" × 54"; *Trip Around the World*, 40" × 50"; and *Dresden Plate*, 38" × 45"; all designed and made by Jerome's family and the staff of *QNM*.

Fireworks Over the City, 56" × 56", designed by Susan Ennis and made by Louise O. Townsend, 1981. Susan combined three blocks called Century of Progress that were originally designed by American quiltmakers for the Century of Progress World's Fair held in Chicago in 1933.

the years to come. Mom, Louise, and Judy were a formidable editorial team, and together they created some of the strongest work that has appeared in *QNM*'s pages over the years.

With enough products on the market to make comparisons, *QNM* undertook product testing of quiltmaking supplies such as fabric, batting, and thread.

Machine quilting was continuing to gain popularity and acceptance and *QNM* began to include quilting designs suitable for continuous machine quilting.

1981

Log Cabin variations abounded in 1981, as quiltmakers experimented with this endlessly versatile design. Penny McMorris saw a dream of two years realized when her television show, *Quilting*, aired on WBGU in Ohio. Reporting on the show in *QNM*, Mom wrote " . . . viewing the program in color was very enjoyable, and we suggest seeking a color TV on which to watch the program." Within two months, 50 stations across the country had signed up to air the thirteen-part series, astonishing the show's producers, but not Penny.

QNM reported on Japanese patchwork pioneer Chuck Nohara and quiltmaking in Japan, which had become wildly popular since being introduced there in the early 1970s.

Mom announced another cover photo contest, and several of the winning photos were

shown together on the cover, a departure from *QNM*'s more typical format of a single quilt, photographed flat. Some of this year's covers even included people in the photograph, including Mom's first grandchild, Jerome DeFelice, looking every bit as adorable as his Uncle Matt had looked twelve years previously. Jerome's sister, Pauline, and his cousins Jessica, Laura, and Eric Bender were the family's new generation of models for many stylish patchwork creations.

The Pat Ferrero documentary *Quilts in Women's Lives* was screened at the landmark "American Quilts: A Handmade Legacy" exhibit at the Oakland Museum. I can personally attest that there were few dry eyes in the house as audiences viewed this powerful, joyous film.

Jeffrey Gutcheon's *QNM* column, "Not For Shopkeepers Only," addressed the concerns of the young but burgeoning quilting industry.

1982

In 1982, editor Marie Shirer and artist Marla Stefanelli joined the magazine staff, and Mom issued a challenge to the staff to envision and outline a concept for a new quilting magazine. Of the proposals and prototypes submitted, Judy Martin's concept for a contemporary pattern magazine was a clear winner. The first issue of *Quiltmaker* was published in April of 1982, and today the magazine has grown into a flourishing and popular resource for quiltmakers.

1981

✳ Linda Reuther and Julie Silber co-curate the show "American Quilts: A Handmade Legacy" at the Oakland Museum in California. The exhibit draws more than 100,000 viewers. ✳ **The Kentucky Quilt Project is undertaken, the first statewide effort to locate and document nineteenth-century quilts, an important part of the state's needlework and artistic heritage.** ✳ The top prizewinner in the second Quilt National is made of paper and plastic, fostering lively discussion.

1982

✳ In response to the growing interest in making patchwork and quilted clothing, several books are published, including Virginia Avery's *Quilts To Wear*, Jean Ray Laury's *Quilted Clothing*, and Yvonne Porcella's *Pieced Clothing Variations*. ✳ **Strip piecing remains wildly popular, although the majority of quiltmakers have not yet realized the suitability of the rotary cutter, introduced in the U.S. in 1980, for this particular technique.**

A proliferation of quilt shows was evident around the country. The *QNM* calendar listed 850 quilt events for the year.

The Lincoln Quilt, 82" × 82", by Laverne Mathews, 1979. Legend has it that Abraham Lincoln's mother, helped by a neighbor, started a quilt in the year of his birth. The pattern for it was finally published in 1942. Laverne customized the pattern with the Trip Around the World coloring.

A very hot topic for quilters was the prevalence of the "cut-'em-up" industry, which fed the public's hunger for vintage patchwork by cutting up antique quilts to make pillows, ornaments, and especially high-fashion garments. (Ralph Lauren's fall 1982 collection included many such jackets, vests, and hostess skirts.) These opportunists didn't cut up damaged quilts and salvage the usable parts as had been done nearly a decade earlier, but instead they bought hundreds of intact antiques at low prices to use as raw material for expensive luxury items. QNM readers reacted strongly to this trend and were even more incensed when the Art Institute of Chicago licensed three of the masterpiece quilts in their collection to be reproduced as poor-quality printed bedspreads. Mom penned some impassioned editorials and inspired many *QNM* readers to express their views to Mr. Lauren and to the Art Institute.

We had outgrown our space again, so Mom and Dad added a two-story addition to our facility. In addition to the magazines, books, catalogs, patterns, and products we manufactured, Mom decided to get into the fabric business. After much mixing of paint and ink we finally captured the colors she envisioned and a local fabric finisher dyed yardages of twelve solid colors of 100-percent cotton, trademarked Columbine Cottons.

Mom was inducted into the Quilters Hall of Fame. Founded in 1979 by Hazel Carter to honor those who have made outstanding contributions to the world of quilting, the Hall of Fame is located in Marie Webster's colonial revival house in Marion, Indiana.

1983 A proliferation of quilt shows was evident around the country. The *QNM* calendar listed 850 quilt events for the year, 128 in the month of October alone. One of the biggest events, A World of Quilts at Meadowbrook Hall in Rochester, Michigan, featured 169 of the finest American, English, and French quilts, displayed in the historic 100-room mansion. Mom was invited to stay at the mansion the night before the show opened, to meander around and enjoy the quilts as much as she wanted. She was surprised to be the only person in the huge, art-filled space that night, and found her stay a bit shadowy and unsettling. The delivery of a McDonald's breakfast the next morning brought her back to reality from an experience she's described as "like being in a Gloria Swanson movie."

Prairie Rose and Pineapple, 90" × 100", maker unknown, around 1860. It is agreed that this quilt was made around 1860, but some attribute it to Massachusetts or Maine, while others feel that it is Midwestern in origin, with elements influenced by New England crewel or embroidery patterns.

Quilt photo by Roy Hale.

Quilt photo courtesy of Cyril I. Nelson, E.P. Dutton & Co.

1983

✳ Quilter Michael James is recognized in two exhibits: "Fabric Constructions: The Art Quilt" and "Michael James: Quiltmaker." Both are displayed in Massachusetts. ✳ **More than 550 quilt guilds are registered in *QNM's International Quilt Guild Directory*.** ✳ Contemporary quilters rediscover crazy quilting and Baltimore Album quilts. ✳ **In his *QNM* column "Not For Shopkeepers Only,"** Jeffrey Gutcheon estimates the value of the 1983 quilt industry to be approximately $750,000,000.

1984

✳ Shadow quilting becomes a popular technique. ✳ **Bill and Meredith Schroeder found the American Quilter's Society in Paducah, Kentucky.** ✳ Julie Silber is named curator of the renowned Esprit collection of Amish quilts. ✳ **The National Quilting Association institutes its Judges Certification Program.** ✳ The first "National Patchwork Championship" is held in England.

QNM's *Special Fifteenth Anniversary Issue*

Red Delicious, 80" × 94", by Connie Powell, 1983. Connie used patterns in *QNM* adapted from the design Apple Patch by Kate Graves of Brandon, Florida. One of *QNM*'s editors, Judy Martin, designed the quilting, and Marie Shirer, another *QNM* editor, made the wallhanging to match the quilt.

Helen Kelley's first "Loose Threads" column appeared in *QNM*, and she began her long relationship with the magazine's readers.

1984 In 1984, *QNM* had its fifteenth anniversary, and we celebrated it with 170,000 of our closest friends, the *QNM* subscribers, by preparing a special commemorative issue.

Developing the *Special Fifteenth Anniversary Issue* was a challenge, but with a talented staff and volunteers we achieved Mom's vision. For a special commemorative cover photo, we set up a picnic/quilting bee scenario in the courtyard of our offices, hanging quilts over the sides of a walkway and two stories of the adjoining building. The quilts were blowing about in the breezy day, causing some consternation. To create the cover shot, my brother Andrew was out of sight on top of the walkway, having thrown his body upon the wires that anchored the upper quilts. His friend Ray Jones, recruited to assist in the effort, tried to look casual in the direct center of the photo while restraining the corners of another pair of billowing quilts. The cake was cardboard, covered with fake icing. As soon as we got the shot we all went back to work.

One of the nicest features of the fifteenth-anniversary issue was the back cover, which Mom devoted to thanking by name (in four-point type) the hundreds of contributors who helped make *QNM* successful (a list I wish we had space to expand and include here).

1985 In 1985, Barbara Brackman continued her series of *QNM* articles offering guidelines for establishing dates for vintage quilts, a valuable reference for quilt collectors and historians.

Ads in the magazine included: a quilter's tour to Ireland; a variety of conferences and seminars; quilt shows and exhibits, including the first American Quilter's Society show; a computer program for figuring yardage; numerous frames and tools; a growing number of shops; a play called *The Quilters*; battings, books, and patterns galore; and ads for other quilting magazines of the day such as *Treadleart*, *Quilt*, *Ladies Circle Patchwork Quilts*, and *Canada Quilts*.

In 1984, *QNM* had its fifteenth anniversary, and we celebrated it with 170,000 of our closest friends.

1985

✳ The American Quilter's Society Show debuts in Paducah, Kentucky. ✳ Ronald McDonald houses, residences for critically ill children undergoing treatment and their families, become a favorite cause of U.S. quiltmakers, and many fund-raising projects and comfort quilts are generated on their behalf. ✳ A growing number of quiltmakers experiment with dyeing and printing their own specialty fabrics.

Fabric advertisements were notably absent, however, as the majority of textile manufacturers were slow to realize the huge potential market of quiltmakers with their endless appetite for wider choices in new fabrics. *QNM* ran an article on this subject, and subsequently published the addresses of the major U.S. manufacturers so that readers could personally express their requests for more variety in fabrics.

1986 This is an excerpt of Mom's editorial letter in the March 1986 issue.

" . . . I would like to use this space to offer a salute to the men beside and behind the women in quilting, and give tribute to one man in particular, whom, I believe, has had great influence on the art and craft of quilting. Without this man's involvement, *Quilter's Newsletter Magazine* likely would not be in your hands right now. Whatever inspiration and direction *QNM* has given to the quilting community over the past 17 years was possible because of his encouragement and participation. I am speaking of my husband, George Leman.

"During the late '60s, when there was little quilting activity and before 'women's lib' had become a household expression, George gave me his unqualified support when I came up with the rather wild idea that I wanted to start a quilting magazine. He did not remind me that I knew very little about publishing, or that there seemed to be no highly visible audience for quilt information. Instead, he expressed confidence that I could do it and asked how he could help.

"As it turned out, he did plenty to help. He took over the responsibility of getting *QNM* printed and mailed each month, and this was after teaching school all day. By 1972 the magazine had outgrown the time and space we had to give it, so he resigned from teaching to help me full-time in nourishing its growth.

"As time went on and he got to know more and more quilters, he became their biggest fan. He admired their patience and persistence in making something of beauty and value—often under adverse circumstances—and he admired their practicality, know-how, and make-it-work spirit.

"He spent a great deal of his time working on ideas and plans for products and services that would in some way make it easier or more convenient for quiltmakers to pursue their quilting. The rest of his time was spent taking care of the business of running the magazine and the office, and taking care of the many everyday problems, so that I could be free to deal with the editorial

Nancy's Garden, 74" × 74", by Nancy Pearson, quilted by Karin Appel, 1983. Nancy adapted several motifs on her appliquéd and embroidered quilt from an anonymous 1845 quilt she saw in *The Quilt Engagement Calendar* (E.P. Dutton, 1981).

Rhythm/Color: Morris Men, 100" × 100", by Michael James, 1985. The quilt is part of a series based on variations on the theme of movement in surface design and dance. The title refers to the colorfully dressed Morris dancers Michael saw in the village streets in Yorkshire and Sussex in England.

1986

✻ New York City hosts the Great American Quilt Festival, which has among its exhibits the winners of the "Statue of Liberty Centennial Contest." A top prize of $20,000 is awarded, a remarkable figure for quilt contests at the time. An estimated 25,000 enthusiastic viewers attend the event.

✻ The first American quilt symposium is held in Japan, featuring classes and lectures by Katie Pasquini, Ruth McDowell, Roberta Horton, Judi Warren, Cheryl Bradkin, and Becky Schaefer. The popularity of quiltmaking in Japan continues to boom.

Nautical Stars, 73" × 88", by Judy Mathieson, 1986. Judy's design was inspired by a 1800's Compass Rose watercolor by an unknown artist she saw in the Greenfield Village/Henry Ford Museum in Michigan. The individual compass blocks were based on ones Judy found on navigational charts, quilt patterns, maps, and hex signs.

The Lotus, 76" × 85", by Bertha Stenge, around 1940. When Bertha made this quilt, she was the best-known quiltmaker of the time. While the blocks are traditional patterns, the border was Bertha's original design.

and artistic details. I would not have been able to bring this magazine nearly so far without his support and help, but with him as a partner it has been an exciting challenge and an adventure.

"George has left us with another challenge now, that of carrying on without him. I know what he would say—'you can do it.' His family and staff will miss him very much, but we will remember his faith and confidence in us, and we shall stride ahead and continue to make QNM grow.

"Body at rest, spirit free.

"George Daniel Leman
December 26, 1927–January 12, 1986"

We still miss him every day.

1987 QNM was made available on newsstands in 1987, and the cover format changed a bit to accommodate text. The methods needed to prepare pages became more complex, as we produced in-house the film used by our printer to make the printing plates. Film preparation was an interesting experience that involved a lot of stinky chemicals and required us to make our print shop environment light-safe. Early on, many a piece of film was ruined when co-workers unwittingly opened the print shop door without noticing the "keep out" sign. In the computer age, this practice now strikes us as comparable to typing all the words twice, but it seemed a natural do-it-yourself solution at the time. We did it as a cost-saving measure so we could afford to print a greater number of QNM pages in color.

Quilt guilds had become a significant component of the quilt world landscape in the late 1980s and QNM published the *International Quilt Guild Directory*, which listed more than 800 quilt guilds worldwide.

String piecing was a popular technique, inspired in part perhaps by the discovery of a significant number of vintage string quilts during various state quilt documentation projects.

The subject of copyright was still on quiltmakers' minds, and Mom once again outlined the restrictions and guidelines of copyright law in her "Needle's Eye" column.

1988 Mom had a wonderful trip to Salzburg, Austria, for the first international

Quilt guilds had become a significant component of the quilt world landscape.

1987
* The San Jose (CA) Quilt Museum moves to a new facility.
* The NQA establishes its Judges Training Program and the National Quilt Registry. * Sotheby's sells an 1840s Baltimore Album quilt for a record sum of $176,000. *
The U.S. puts an embargo on the importation of greige goods (raw cotton fabric). Quiltmakers see price increases and changes in quality. * Cleve Jones and friends form the NAMES project, organizing the collection and display of quilt block panels commemorating victims of AIDS.

1988
* Organized by the American/International Quilt Association and Quilts, Inc., the first international quilt conference, Quilt Expo Europa, takes place in Salzburg, Austria. *
African-American quilting receives recognition in a number of museum exhibits including venues such as the Hunter Museum of Art in Tennessee, and the San Francisco Craft and Folk Art Museum. * Quiltmaking trends of the day include charm quilts and a variety of Log Cabin variations.

quilting conference, International Quilt Expo Europa, organized by the American/International Quilt Association (later known as the International Quilt Association or IQA). Mom found a warm welcome among the European quilters who were familiar with the magazine (QNM had subscribers in fifty-six countries by this time) and formed lasting friendships. QNM sponsored Visions of the World, the international competition that was displayed there. Mom and the other judges felt the quality of work in the entries for this contest surpassed any previous QNM competition.

That year, on a visit to Russia, President and Mrs. Reagan presented a quilt to Premier and Mrs. Gorbachev at the Moscow summit meetings. Its maker, Julia Spidell, duplicated the original quilt *Peace Baskets*, and this second quilt appeared on the cover of QNM's January 1989 cover.

Mom was designing fabric again, and we were producing books, patterns, and other products at a pretty fast clip. By the time our 200th issue was published, our print run each month had exceeded 200,000 copies.

1989

At the American Quilter's Society show the winner of the Best of Show award was entirely machine pieced and quilted, causing a temporary furor.

Hand-dyed and hand-painted cottons began to find popularity with mainstream quilters, and Baltimore Album quilts enjoyed the beginnings of a revival. Metallic threads and fabrics became available on the market.

Patterns in QNM were typically presented using traditional template construction, with readers expected to add their own ¼" seam allowance, although rotary cutting finally began to be accepted by quiltmakers.

1990

It was a busy year, as Mom traveled to Odense, Denmark, for the second International Quilt Expo Europa. QNM once again sponsored a competition that was on exhibit at the show. The countries represented had grown to include quilters from most of the European nations, Asia, the Pacific Rim, North America, South America, and Africa. A little more than a week after Mom's trip, the Quilts, Inc.-sponsored Spring Quilt Market and Festival opened in Denver. We spruced up our offices, and hung quilts from our company quilt collection as well as quilts made by our editorial and art staff. We were happy to offer hourly tours of our workspace during the Festival, but there was more interest than we anticipated. We could only accommodate groups of fifty people per tour, and during those three days in May it felt as if most of the 5,000-plus Festival attendees had stopped by our offices.

Sewing machine manufacturers began to advertise in the pages of QNM, perhaps realizing that many quiltmakers were making quilts by machine rather than by hand.

Quilt photo courtesy of Elly Sienkiewicz.

Friendship's Offering, 113" × 113", made by fifty-four friends of Sue Hannan, and quilted by Emma and Fannie Hershberger, 1987. For her seventieth birthday, Sue's friends made blocks with designs taken from an 1847 album quilt made by Sarah Holcombe. Elly Sienkiewicz designed the border.

Twentieth Anniversary Issue. To celebrate the twentieth anniversary, the September issues from each year that QNM was in publication are shown on this cover, beginning at the bottom left corner and progressing clockwise around the page. The Lone Star in the center was made by QNM staff in 1975.

1989

✳ More than 1,200 quiltmakers worldwide submit entries to the "Memories of Childhood" contest organized by the Museum of American Folk Art, and the winning quilt takes home a prize of $7,500. The finalist quilts are displayed with other special exhibits at the Great American Quilt Festival 2 in New York City. ✳ **Barbara Brackman predicts that the last quarter of the twentieth century will come to be known as the golden age of quiltmaking, a time of unparalleled growth, variety, and excellent workmanship.**

1990

✳ The second Quilt Expo Europa is held in Denmark, as quiltmaking continues to capture international enthusiasm. ✳ **The National Quilting Association institutes the first National Quilting Day.** ✳ Mancuso Show Management holds the first Mid-Atlantic Quilt Festival, and the organizers go on to produce several large annual shows at venues across the U.S. ✳ **The Baltimore Album revival is well under way, fostering great interest in fancy appliqué and dimensional appliqué techniques.**

Have You Ever Seen Flowers in the Ocean?, 59" × 64", by Keiko Goke, 1989. Keiko's textured quilt won the top award for creativity in innovative design in *QNM*'s second international competition. Delicate hand embroidery in a variety of stitches enhances the sinuous curves of the piece.

Peacocks, 82" × 82", by Dixie McBride, 1990. Dixie hand-delivered this quilt to *QNM*'s offices for photography. Hand pieced, appliquéd, and quilted, this quilt marked the beginning of Dixie's long association as a contributor to *QNM*.

QNM sponsored the "Home Sweet Home" block contest and received nearly 1,000 entries from all over the world.

1991 Ongoing research findings about nineteenth- and twentieth-century African-American quilting continued to gain recognition for these unique works as examples not only of art, craft, and family heritage, but as social and cultural commentary expressed in cloth.

The well-established presence of quilt guilds and conferences had in turn contributed to a new career choice in quilting—that of the traveling quilt teacher and lecturer.

Lured by the healthy American appetite for all things quilted, some overseas manufacturers begin to produce "hand-stitched heirloom quilts" in China among other places. These poorly made quilts retailed for about $65, leading quiltmakers to an educated guess that the workers were toiling for pennies, and causing concern that the work required to make a true heirloom quilt would be undervalued once again by the general public.

By this time, the growth of Leman Publications, which consisted of *Quilter's Newsletter Magazine*, *Quiltmaker*, Moon Over the Mountain (a book publishing division), and Quilts & Other Comforts (our retail catalog business), had exceeded Mom's wildest imagination. Managing the business needs of the company

and a staff of fifty had become so time-consuming that they conflicted with the time Mom could spend writing and developing articles for *QNM*. My sisters Megan and Georgianne still worked at the company, but the rest of my siblings had gone on to pursue other careers. For some time, another larger, family-owned magazine publishing company had expressed interest in buying Leman Publications, and by the end of the year we had become a subsidiary.

1992 The concern about overseas-made, mass-produced "heirloom quilts" was compounded when it was learned that the Smithsonian Institution had sold the licensing rights on the 300-plus historic quilts in its collection to a housewares importer. Poorly made imports of four of the finest nineteenth-century quilts in their collection were being offered for sale in the U.S.

Mom encouraged her readers to speak up and thousands of outraged quiltmakers wrote to the Smithsonian, their congressmen, then-Senator Al Gore, the *Washington Post*, and the American companies selling these quilts through their catalogs and stores. CNN covered the determined quiltmakers who marched in protest on the National Mall. The House Appropriations Committee launched an investigation into the licensing matter and Mom met with the Smithsonian officials in Washington to pass on the point of view of *QNM* readers. Karey Bresenhan, of Quilts, Inc., along with several representatives of the National Quilting Asso-

1991

✳ The Daughters of the American Revolution (DAR) Museum renovates its exhibit space to display more of its collection. Detailed origins and family history accompany more than half of the 400-plus quilts and coverlets. ✳ **Nebraska quiltmakers organize a truly statewide quilt show, with seventeen separate exhibits at destinations along Interstate 80, which spans the state from east to west.** ✳ Fabric manufacturers begin to invite various well-known quiltmakers and designers to create signature fabric lines.

1992

✳ The rotary cutter finally begins to find acceptance with mainstream quiltmakers, and strip-piecing techniques including Seminole patchwork are popular. ✳ **The NQA successfully petitions Congress to declare a National Quilting Day to be held yearly on the third Saturday in March.** ✳ The Smithsonian's National Museum of American History sells licensing rights for the quilts in the Institution's collection and American quilters express their outrage.

ciation, the Continental Quilting Congress, and the American Quilt Study Group, spoke on behalf of the quilt industry. By the end of the meetings, the Smithsonian promised more accurate labeling of the imports and that all royalties earned from sales of the quilts be dedicated to the textile division of the Institution.

The manufacturing company producing the imported knockoffs saw their yearly income increase from $15 million to $100 million on the strength of the sales of the Smithsonian reproductions. By the end of 1992, as reported in QNM, reproductions of more than 200 different classic American quilts were being mass-produced overseas and imported to the U.S.

1993

The growing use of the Internet spawned an interesting new activity for quiltmakers: fabric swaps with quilting friends around the country and the world. They coined the term "squishies" for the packages of swap fabric they received in the mail.

QNM readers kept up their letter-writing campaign to the Smithsonian. Karey Bresenhan and Nancy O'Bryant of Quilts, Inc. organized a grassroots petition drive capturing tens of thousands of signatures that they presented to museum representatives. They suggested ways the museum could benefit financially from its quilt collection that would not conflict with the American quilt industry. The Smithsonian agreed to authorize only American manufacture of reproductions of

the quilts, and the first such arrangement was made with the Cabin Creek Quilters cooperative in Malden, West Virginia.

1994

1994 was QNM's twenty-fifth anniversary year. In her April editorial letter, Mom remarked that if anyone had suggested back in 1969 that someday we'd be designing quilts on computers and talking about them on television, she would have thought it a joke.

The Smithsonian Institution stayed in the forefront of quilters' awareness, this time in a better way. They reached an agreement with RJR Fashion Fabrics for the reproduction of a number of fabrics found in the early nineteenth-century quilts in their collection. Everybody won—the Smithsonian could generate needed revenue from its collection, and quiltmakers would have a wonderful new range of fabric choices. Jinny Beyer and Bonnie Benn Stratton were members of the selection committee that viewed the quilts and chose the fabrics to be reproduced, and Mom and Karey Bresenhan observed the process. This agreement became a model that is now frequently practiced by a number of museums and fabric manufacturers.

In the fall, our whole family—husbands, kids, and many of the QNM staff attended the International Quilt Festival in Houston, where we proudly watched Mom receive the first Silver Star award. (The Silver Star is an annual industry award, instituted by Karey Bresenhan of

Inclined Log Cabin, 70" × 70", by Keiko Goke, 1991. An innovative take on a traditional pattern earned Best of Show honors for Keiko in QNM's contest "Quilts: Discovering a New World." Entries to the contest were displayed at Quilt Expo Europa III in The Netherlands in 1992.

Cosmic Distance, 93" × 93", by Keiko Takahashi, 1990. Keiko's careful piecing and airbrushed gold and silver stars earned her a place in the annual "Hands All Around" invitational exhibit, sponsored by QNM, at the 1992 International Quilt Festival in Houston, Texas.

1993

✳ The Alliance For American Quilts is formed to ensure that American quilts are recognized in art and history. Plans include the International Quilt Index and the American Quilt History Center. ✳ The Museum of American Folk Art announces the Great American Quilt Festival, formerly a biennial event, will take place annually. ✳ The New England Quilt Museum in Lowell, Massachusetts, is awarded $55,000 in grants to help relocate after flood damage the previous year.

1994

✳ The first European Patchwork Meeting is held in France. ✳ The Maryland Historical Society exhibits more than two dozen never-before-displayed nineteenth-century Baltimore Album quilts from its collection. ✳ The Knoxville Museum of Art sponsors the traveling exhibit "Patchwork Souvenirs of the 1933 World's Fair" consisting of quilts entered into the 1933 quilt contest at the Chicago World's Fair. ✳ Online quilt guilds become an increasingly popular way for quilters to share their interests.

QNM's *Silver Anniversary Quilt*, 100" × 100", designed by Annie Tregay Segal, pieced by Penny Wolf, quilted by Jonna Castle, 1994. Adapted from a traditional Indian Wedding Ring pattern, stars were added to the intersections. The fabrics include a print with silver and silver quilting thread was used in honor of the occasion.

Kauai: Holiday Greetings, 78" × 86", by Moneca Calvert, 1994. Well-known for her innovative machine piecing, this quilt commemorates a stay in Hawaii, and depicts the huge double-headed native poinsettias that grow on the islands.

Quilts, Inc., given in recognition of work that contributed a lasting influence on the quilt world.) Mom spoke movingly about her experiences in founding and running QNM, and in her typical modest fashion gave the credit for QNM's success more to luck and timing than to her own hard work, vision, and creativity. When she recognized and thanked Dad for his support and contributions it was a poignant moment, as the day of the awards ceremony would have been their fortieth wedding anniversary. The next day at another event, I was thrilled that the anniversary quilt we had been making secretly for a year was a complete surprise when we presented it to Mom. Many of her longtime friends, as well as all our family, had contributed blocks. She loved it.

QNM began a series of articles by Carter Houck showcasing various museum quilt collections. Public and institutional consciousness had been raised regarding the artistic and cultural significance of quilts, and museums were beginning to display the quilts in their possession more frequently.

1995 Early in the year, we were surprised by the results of a survey we had commissioned. In partnership with Quilts, Inc., QNM had undertaken a study to investigate the size of the American quilting community. While we knew it was a very healthy industry with a large audience, we had never speculated that there might be more than 15.5 million quilters in the U.S., as the survey indicated.

Across the country, full-page ads appeared in newspapers, especially in rural areas, announcing local two- and three-day quilt evaluation events, encouraging owners of vintage quilts to "sell those old unwanted family quilts to help preserve them." In actuality these faux preservationists bought old quilts, and then took them to other areas of the country where they were resold at higher prices. Many family heirlooms were lost to this scheme, and state heritage projects lost out as well.

We moved our offices again and our new space was easily four times the size of our previous facility. Much of it was devoted to a huge warehouse for our by-then greatly expanded Quilts & Other Comforts mail-order operations. We also gained a lovely gallery space for revolving quilt exhibits, to which visitors are still welcome, here in Golden, Colorado.

1996 Our fifth international competition was held, and the theme Mom came up with inspired many quilters. "Quilts: Artistic Expressions" was the most popular contest we'd ever organized. Hundreds of works were entered, and the quilts were spectacular. The resulting exhibit pleased crowds at Quilt Expo V in France, as well as at the International Quilt Festival in Houston that year.

In the summer of 1996, Mom decided that it was time to retire. In the September issue she shared with her readers how much she had enjoyed her job over the past twenty-seven

1995

✳ *How to Make an American Quilt*, based on Whitney Ottos's best-selling book, is the first movie to feature a quilt in a starring role. ✳ Paper-foundation piecing is a new technique for quiltmakers and watercolor quilts are a popular new style. ✳ Nancy Crow is the first quilt artist to have an exhibit of her work in the prestigious Renwick Gallery of the Smithsonian Institution.

1996

✳ All of the panels of the AIDS Memorial Quilt go on display together for the last time. ✳ Machine quilting begins to find wide acceptance among mainstream traditional quiltmakers as well as their contemporary counterparts. Longarm machines are relatively new on the market, as are a handful of quilt design software programs. ✳ A handful of quilt-themed fiction begins to be available. Primarily mysteries, these are very popular with who-done-it-loving quiltmakers.

years, and gave her heartfelt thanks to them for all their friendship and support. Mom had asked me to try to fill her shoes, and while I was not at all convinced that this was a good idea, I agreed. Unlike Mom, I am not a writer. I tried every conceivable ploy to get out of having to write the monthly editorial letter. I thought the first one would kill me, but it has gotten a little easier over time, and hopefully the readers have gotten used to it, too.

1997 It was a challenging year, as we adjusted to producing QNM without Mom's daily guidance. I freely admit to requesting lots of her input in that first year, a luxury I still enjoy. Fortunately for the readers and me, QNM had a strong staff that included editors Jeannie Spears, Marie Shirer, Vivian Ritter, Barbara Smith, and Kay Jesse. Art director Kathryn Wagar Wright ably led the creative team of artists Annie Segal, Debbe Benson, Joyce Robinson, and photographer Mellisa Karlin Mahoney. I will never forget the patience and support this team gave me as I tackled new responsibilities.

Quiltmakers were embracing all kinds of fun new methods: painting fabrics, working with specialty threads, fabric photo transfers and mixed media embellishments, experimenting with a variety of dyeing and surface manipulation techniques, beading, and silk ribbon embroidery. Water-soluble stabilizers and a variety of fusible products had opened up exciting new possibilities. Traditionalists rediscovered

redwork, and old-time embroidery patterns were very popular. Quilters still couldn't seem to get enough tone-on-tone fabrics, especially with natural textural themes such as botanicals, sky, water, stone, and wood.

In the pages of QNM, advertisements for on-line retailers and quilt design software proliferated, computers and computerization having become an established part of the quiltmaking universe.

QNM ran a short series of articles on quilt show judging practices. The quilt world had changed considerably since QNM first published Mom's judge's scorecard in 1977; it was widely agreed that contemporary quiltmaking defied some of the categorizations that applied to earlier generations of quilted works.

1998 In 1998, we published a notice seeking charter subscribers of QNM—those quilters who had subscribed continuously since the first issue in 1969. We were very happy to hear from twenty-seven such long-time readers, and the "Quilting Bee" in QNM's 300th issue introduced several of them to the rest of our readers.

Later that year, the publishing company that had wooed us so successfully back in 1991 decided that our operation no longer suited its business plans, and it was announced to the staff that our company was for sale. We carried on, producing the best magazines and catalogs

Autumn Basket, 98" × 98", by Shoko Ferguson, 1995. Shoko made a miniature version of this quilt to try out her ideas before she began work on the full-size quilt, a practice she often employs. Shoko tried to capture the feeling of brisk autumn breezes in this piece.

Willow, 75" × 75", by Jane A. Sassaman, 1996. Jane made this quilt for her then twelve-year-old daughter, Willow. The original influence for this machine appliquéd, machine pieced quilt was found in a photo of a seventeenth-century embroidered Elizabethan jacket.

1997

✴ Embellishment of all kinds continues to grow in popularity with contemporary quiltmakers who are experimenting with raw-edge surfaces, thread painting, dimensional techniques, and mixed media quilts. ✴ Robert and Ardis James of Chappaqua, New York, donate a museum-quality quilt collection valued at more than $6 million to the University of Nebraska-Lincoln. In addition, they underwrite the establishment of the International Quilt Study Center at the university.

1998

✴ The Quilter's Heritage Celebration in Lancaster, Pennsylvania, is named one of the top 100 attractions in the U.S. by the American Bus and Motorcoach Association. ✴ Three of America's best-loved early-twentieth-century quiltmakers, Marie Webster, Rose Kretsinger, and Carrie Hall, have their masterpiece quilts displayed in Tokyo, Japan. Also in Japan this year, World Quilt '98 welcomes more than 100,000 visitors. The event celebrates the thirtieth anniversary of Tadanobu Seto's Japan Handicrafts Association.

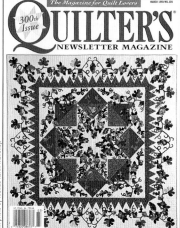

Days of Wine and Roses, 76" × 77", by Deborah Grow. 1997. For its 300th issue, *QNM* wanted something special, and Deborah's quilt fit the bill. Deborah combined two appliqué patterns from well-known designer Nancy Pearson with designs of her own.

Earthly Delights, 81" × 81", by Karen Kay Buckley, 1999. Karen used hand appliqué techniques to create this exuberant and elegant design that was inspired by the work of nineteenth-century German textile designer Friedrich Fishbach.

we could as we awaited a resolution and answers about whom our new owner might be.

Soon, Quilts & Other Comforts, the little business that had started it all, was sold off to Clotilde, the well-known sewing catalog company. After the salable inventory had been shipped to the new owners, we cleaned out the cavernous warehouse of nearly thirty years' worth of odds and ends. It was disheartening to see box after box of back issues discarded in the trash. Afterwards, we dearly missed having shelf upon shelf of the latest fabrics to choose from when making up samples or working on new quilt designs, not to mention the chance to try out the newest quilting tools and gadgets. Today, Quilts & Other Comforts is owned and successfully operated by Suzan Ellis, who had been our marketing manager for many years.

A few days prior to the signing of the final paperwork that would transfer ownership of QNM to Primedia, our new publishers, one of our soon-to-be-former owners traveled to our offices to take possession of the majority of our extensive company quilt collection. It consisted of hundreds of quilts that we had made, commissioned, been given, or purchased over the previous thirty years. I displayed the quilts one by one and related the history of each before they were folded and taken away.

1999 The staffs of QNM and *Quiltmaker* welcomed our new sister publications

McCall's Quilting, and *Quick Quilts* (existing Primedia publications) to our Colorado offices. It was *QNM*'s thirtieth birthday that year, and we were involved in a contest that generated powerful and emotive quilts. In conjunction with the International Quilt Study Center, we had sponsored the "Quilts: Expressions of Freedom" contest and exhibit, and the finalists hailed from Canada, Chile, Costa Rica, England, France, Germany, Holland, India, Israel, Japan, Latvia, Norway, Russia, and the U.S. The theme of this competition was the celebration of human rights.

The previous fall, Karey Bresenhan and Nancy O'Bryant had proposed an exciting and challenging project—the Ultimate Quilt Search—to identify the 100 best quilts made in the twentieth century, and to gather them for a once-in-a-lifetime display as we approached the turn of the millennium. Representatives of the four most influential not-for-profit quilt organizations—The National Quilting Association, the American Quilt Study Group, the International Quilt Association, and the Alliance For American Quilts Inc. nominated and reviewed hundreds of quilts. Their hard work paid off at one of the most significant quilt exhibitions of the twentieth century.

The "Twentieth Century's Best American Quilts" exhibit was shown at the Silver Anniversary of the International Quilt Festival. The quilts were breathtaking individually and collectively, and inspired hushed reverence and high emotions in thousands of viewers. QNM was honored to participate in the

---

1999

✸ Scientific studies had shown that sewing could reduce stress and lower blood pressure. A new study shows that sewing can increase self-esteem, creativity, and problem-solving skills for children 8–12 years old. ✸ More quilt shops and individuals begin to offer longarm machine quilting services. Fusibles are accepted as a method for appliqué, and other embellishment treatments for quilts are explored. ✸ Luanne Boles Becker's documentary *Unraveling the Stories: Quilts as a Reflection of Our Lives* is nominated for an Emmy.

2000

✸ Manufacturers introduce new products to transfer photos onto fabric using a computer. The Electric Quilt Company introduces software that incorporates printable files of the latest fabrics. More online retailers offer a wide variety of products and services for quilters. ✸ P&B Fabrics organizes and underwrites "Quilts Over Kosovo," and more than 5,000 quilts are made and shipped to families in the war-torn area, often accompanied by letters of compassion written by the individual quiltmakers.

search and in developing the commemorative exhibit catalog.

Silver Star winners of the previous five years each curated a special exhibit at the Festival and Mom selected the category of traditional quilts. Mom also began a series of articles for QNM's 30th birthday in the September 1999 issue, recalling a few of her fondest memories of her adventures in the world of quilts and publishing.

2000 The year 2000 arrived and the lights stayed on. Many remarkable quilts were made to commemorate the transition of the millennium.

Mom continued her retrospective of the twentieth-century quilt revival for QNM, and we all enjoyed the trip down memory lane as she recounted it from an insider's viewpoint.

For quilters, the term UFO had taken on a new meaning, having nothing to do with Roswell or aliens. UFOs are UnFinished Objects, an unfortunate side effect of starting more quilt projects than one can reasonably finish in a lifetime.

The issues of copyright and credit continued to bedevil quiltmakers. Perhaps in part because of the long tradition quilters had of freely sharing patterns and knowledge, some companies in the quilt industry as well as individual quilters have a hard time distinguishing between copy-right violations and sharing. With the increase of commissioned machine quilting on quilts entered into competitions, show organizers found they needed to be more vigilant in proper accreditation in programs and signage.

The International Quilt Expo VI took place in Strasbourg, France, and the finalists and winning quilts in our seventh international competition, "Quilts: Crossing Boundaries," were exhibited there.

With quilt design software and pattern libraries on CD becoming more popular than ever, we got on the bandwagon by choosing more than 170 projects from QNM's 1995–2000 issues and compiling them onto a CD. Translating our printed pages into electronic format was quite a learning experience.

2001 By 2001, sewing machine manufacturers had made some amazing advances in technology. The new models often boasted computers that could be programmed for a variety of functions, and many featured a wide variety of preprogrammed embroidery stitches and motifs. Other machines, more specifically for quiltmakers, were designed with a roomier work area for piecing and quilting.

I was honored when asked to join the advisory board of the International Quilt Study Center, and got my first chance to see the world's largest public quilt collection at the annual meeting, held at the University of Nebraska-Lincoln.

Bristol Stars, 81" × 81", by Judy Mathieson, 1999. As one of the quiltmakers represented in The *Twentieth Century's Best American Quilts*, Judy is well known for her Mariner's Compass designs. This quilt was inspired by a Victorian marble floor in the Bristol Cathedral in England.

Crazy Stars, 83" × 81", by Amy Bucher, 1885. This vibrantly graphic quilt is in the unparalleled quilt collection of the International Quilt Study Center at the University of Nebraska-Lincoln. This quilt is reportedly made of leftover scraps from two other quilts made by Amy.

2001

✴ Another *Quilting In America* survey indicates the quilt world as a whole has grown even more than expected, with an estimated industry value of $1.8 billion. ✴ The Vermont Quilt Festival celebrates its twenty-fifth anniversary under the leadership of founder Richard Cleveland. ✴ $500,000 in damages is awarded to a quiltmaker for copyright violation against a manufacturer of reproduction quilts. The same company reaches an out-of-court settlement with Jinny Beyer, whose internationally-known copyrighted quilt *Ray of Light* had been illegally reproduced by the thousands. As part of the settlement, almost 4,000 unsold quilts are donated to Habitat for Humanity. ✴ The world changes on September 11, and a powerful and moving exhibit of quilts made in the days and weeks following the attacks is displayed at the International Quilt Festival.

Christmas in the Forest, 78" × 83", by Kathy McNeil, 2001. Kathy used her husband as her model for the Father Christmas figure. She used many different techniques such as crazy quilting, paper piecing, color-wash, and hand and machine appliqué to assemble the quilt.

Old Glory, 91" × 93", by Janet Fogg, 2002. The machine piecing of this quilt was well underway when the terrorist attacks of September 11th occurred, and Janet felt even more strongly compelled to finish and exhibit her work as quickly as possible to display her patriotic feelings.

The tragic events of September 11, 2001, shocked and affected the world, and quiltmakers turned to their quilting not only for solace but to express the inexpressible. At the twenty-seventh International Quilt Festival that October, the most significant exhibit was "AMERICA: From the Heart," a gathering of almost 300 quilts made in response to the events of September 11. Made in the days after the attack, many of the quilts were powerfully heart-wrenching; others conveyed a deep sense of peace or patriotism. The logistics and planning required to mount this exhibit so shortly after the tragedy are a testament to the dedication of the quiltmakers and the many volunteers who assisted in the endeavor. This quilt exhibit was without a doubt one of the most important that will take place in the twenty-first century.

2002 The first weeks and months of 2002 found quiltmakers still responding to the attacks in New York, Pennsylvania, and Washington, D.C., in a variety of ways, including making fund-raising quilts, creating comfort quilts for the victims' families, and organizing a variety of commemorative projects.

The documentary *A Century of Quilts: America in Cloth* was broadcast on PBS networks nationwide. The program offered a video tour of the 1999 exhibit "The Twentieth Century's Best American Quilts," and included interviews with some of the living quilt artists whose work was named on the list of the century's best.

QNM editors Jan Magee and Vivian Ritter traveled to Japan to attend the first Tokyo International Great Quilt Festival, where QNM had a major exhibit on display. It went into the record books as the largest quilt show ever, with more than 245,000 visitors. Later that year, I too visited Tokyo to judge the competition for the second International Great Quilt Festival. All three of us found that the friendliness and enthusiasm of the Japanese quiltmakers we met helped to transcend any language or cultural barriers. One of the most popular exhibits there was "Thirty Distinguished Quiltmakers," an invitational showcase of contemporary quiltmaking, organized by QNM and curated by Robert Shaw.

The Alliance For American Quilts launched its website, the Center For The Quilt Online (www.centerforthequilt.org). One feature on the site, Quilt Treasures, presented filmed interviews with notable individuals who had significantly contributed to the twentieth-century quilt revival. Noted researcher and author Cuesta Benberry was one of the first interviewees, as was Mom. I was there for the taping of Mom's interview, and we had a great time, along with interviewer Marsha MacDowell.

2003 In 2003, several major exhibits drew international attention, including the display of the fine quilt collection of Shelburne Museum in Vermont and the inspirational "Quilts of Gee's Bend," a collection of African-American quilts.

2002

✳ Quilting, introduced to Korea in the 1980s, has become a popular pastime there, and as has happened in many other countries, Korean quiltmakers combine elements of their own textile and design heritage with traditional American quilt styles to produce works unique to their culture. ✳ Robert and Ardis James donate the *Reconciliation Quilt*, which had been auctioned by Sotheby's in 1991 for a record price of $264,000 to the International Quilt Study Center. ✳ The Freedom Bee of Alberta, Alabama, celebrates its thirty-fifth anniversary. ✳ The American textile industry finds itself affected once again as U.S. environmental regulations make the manufacturing and finishing processes required for cotton fabrics significantly more costly to produce in the U.S. than overseas. More than 100 U.S. textile plants close as a result of the increase in offshore fabric production.

The long tradition of pro bono quiltmaking was stronger than ever, with quiltmakers turning out comfort quilts and organizing fund-raisers for all types of children's groups, refugees of war, victims of violence, those in the armed services, patients battling illness, and others in need.

QNM commissioned the third industry survey, *Quilting in America 2003* and in a joint project with International Quilt Study Center and the International Quilt Association, QNM helped underwrite research into the effects of aging on adhesive and fusible materials commonly used in quiltmaking.

The QNM staff began making plans for the magazine's thirty-fifth birthday in 2004. The magazine announced its newest international contest, and we looked forward with anticipation to the coming year.

TO BE CONTINUED . . .

The quilt world has grown more than anyone could have imagined back in 1969.

There's now a bounty of information available for quilters, with many magazines and dozens of new books every year. U.S. and international quilt events now number in the hundreds annually. More than twenty major U.S. shows display hundreds of quilts, and the still-growing quilt industry has created more tools and notions than most dedicated quiltmakers could use in a lifetime.

Traveling quilt teachers and lecturers are regularly hosted at guild meetings and quilt shops, and merchant's malls are fixtures of most annual guild shows. By a conservative industry estimate, there are more than 3,000 independently-owned quilt shops in the U.S.

Quiltmaking is flourishing internationally, with the life experience, culture, and natural surroundings of the individual makers reflected in their quilts, creating unique works and new traditions.

By the end of 2003, QNM had, over the years, published 19,078 pages packed with inspiration, information, and imagination. We've mailed QNM to subscribers in more than 100 countries, from Abu Dhabi to Zimbabwe. Mom still compares putting together the magazine to the making of a paper quilt, and her goal was always to stitch the parts together into a pleasing, comforting whole. We've tried to carry on her vision, and to keep the vows she made in 1970, when she resolved to do her "... best to make QNM the best magazine there is or ever was for quilters . . ." As we head into the future, our warmest regards go out to our loyal and supportive readers and contributors, as they have since 1969, when Mom put together, on our kitchen table, the very first issue of "The Magazine For Quilt Lovers."

Wishing you Happy Quilting from everyone at *Quilter's Newsletter Magazine* —

—Mary Leman Austin

Quilt photo by Mellisa Karlin Mahoney.

For the Celests, 73" × 73", by Sandi McMillan ,1999. The color plan of this quilt, as well as the design, expresses the maker's view of the highs and lows experienced by women whose lives have been touched by breast cancer. The central star represents someone taking up the fight against the disease, surrounded by a circle of support represented by the smaller stars. This award-winning quilt is machine pieced, hand appliquéd, and machine quilted.

2003

※ The International Quilt Study Center acquires the notable Holstein/van der Hoof quilt collection, a group of 400 quilts that includes the very same works that had contributed to the recognition of quilts as art, way back in 1971. ※ Vandalism to two quilts hanging at the International Quilt Festival results in arrest and a six-month prison sentence for the perpetrator. ※ The Whitney Museum of American Art in New York hosts an exhibit of quilts made in Gee's Bend, Alabama. The quilts, striking examples of improvisational construction and artistry as well as community tradition, go on to be shown at many other museums around the country, winning national acclaim. Many of the quiltmakers represented in the exhibit were members of the original Freedom Bee, established in 1966.

Projects

OVER THE YEARS many wonderful quilts have appeared on the cover of Quilter's Newsletter Magazine. Here are fifteen of those cover quilts that you can make yourself.

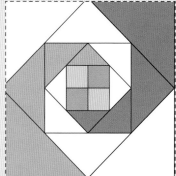

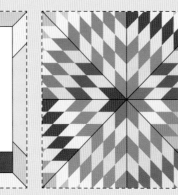

Chaco's Paw

LAURIE EVANS

Laurie Evans of Austin, Texas, made the bright and cheerful Chaco's Paw. *The quilt was patterned after a late-1800s Bear's Paw variation. The designer noted that while she was piecing this traditional design, a new kitten named Chaco came to live with her. Since he was such a help in the piecing of this quilt, she decided to name the quilt for him.*

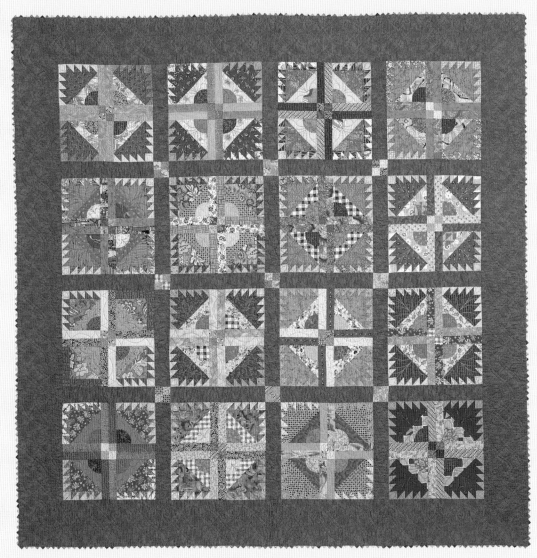

Made by Laurie Evans.

Materials and Cutting

BLOCK SIZE: 15" × 15"

QUILT SIZE: 81" × 81"

- ◆ Requirements are based on 42" fabric width.
- ◆ Borders include 2" extra length plus seam allowances. Measure your top and cut to size.
- ◆ Read all instructions before cutting.

MATERIALS	YARDS	CUTTING
Assorted Light Scraps	1⅜	
(behind "paws")		512 D patches, 64 E patches
Assorted Bright Scraps	5	64 A patches, 64 B patches, 64 C patches, 512 D patches,
		100 E patches, 128 F patches
Blue Solid	3⅛	
borders		4 at 7¼" × 83½"
sashing		24 G patches
Assorted Bright Scraps	¾	
prairie points*		324 squares 1½" × 1½"
Binding*	¾	9 strips 2½" × 42"
Backing	5	3 panels 29" × 85"
Batting		85" × 85"

*Choose between prairie points and binding.

✦ **tips** The quilt shown contains approximately 95 prairie points per side. Instructions are given for 81 prairie points per side—these slightly larger points are easier to handle and position.

To make turning under the seam allowances of the backing easier, sew ¼" in from the edges all around the backing and use the stitching as a guide when turning under the seam allowance.

Optional binding materials are also included.

For patches C, D, and E you can either rotary cut the squares, then cut them diagonally in half where indicated or you can make triangle templates. Both are given on page 32.

Getting Started

Wash and press fabrics. Cut the patches and borders as listed in the materials and cutting box. Refer to pages 104–107 for Quilting Basics.

Making the Blocks

1 Join A, B, C, D, E, and F patches to make a Bear's Paw block, referring to Block Piecing.

2 Make 16 blocks.

3 Join 4 E patches to make a setting square.

4 Make 9 setting squares.

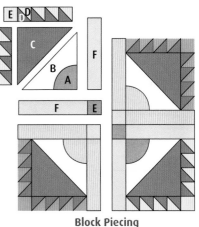

Block Piecing
Make 16.

Assembling the Quilt Top

1 Join 4 blocks and 3 G sashing pieces for each block row, beginning with a block and alternating blocks and sashing pieces. Press seam allowances toward sashing.

2 Make 4 block rows.

3 Join 4 sashing pieces and 3 setting squares to make a sashing row, beginning with a sashing piece and alternating sashing pieces and setting squares. Press seam allowances toward sashing.

4 Make 3 sashing rows.

5 Join block rows and sashing rows, beginning with a block row and alternating block rows and sashing rows. Press seam allowances in one direction.

6 Sew the borders to the sides of the quilt, referring to the mitered corner borders section of Quilting Basics on pages 104–105. Sew the borders to the top and bottom. Press the seam allowances toward the borders.

7 Miter the corners.

Quilting and Finishing

1 Mark the quilt top with quilting motifs as desired.

2 Layer and baste the quilt backing, batting, and top.

3 Quilt the motifs as marked, quilting no closer than 1" from the outer edge of the quilt, to allow for the backing to be folded out of the way while the prairie points are sewn to the quilt top.

4 Make individual prairie points by folding each 1½" × 1½" square in half diagonally, then in half again. Press the folds.

Making prairie points

5 Fold the quilt backing out of the way.

6 Trim quilt batting even with the quilt top.

7 Work on the front side of the quilt top and position 81 prairie points along each side of the quilt, aligning the raw edges of the prairie points with the raw edges of the quilt top and spacing the prairie points 1 per inch along the seamline. The 2 points at the corners should just meet. Note that the prairie points will overlap in the seam allowance.

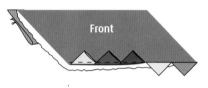

8 Sew through the prairie points, the quilt top, and the batting, using a ¼" seam allowance. After sewing around all sides, fold the prairie points out from the quilt top and press.

9 Turn under a ¼" seam allowance on the backing around the perimeter of the quilt and hand sew backing in place along the prairie points on the back side of the quilt, as shown.

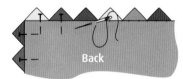

Align arrows with lengthwise or crosswise grain of fabric.

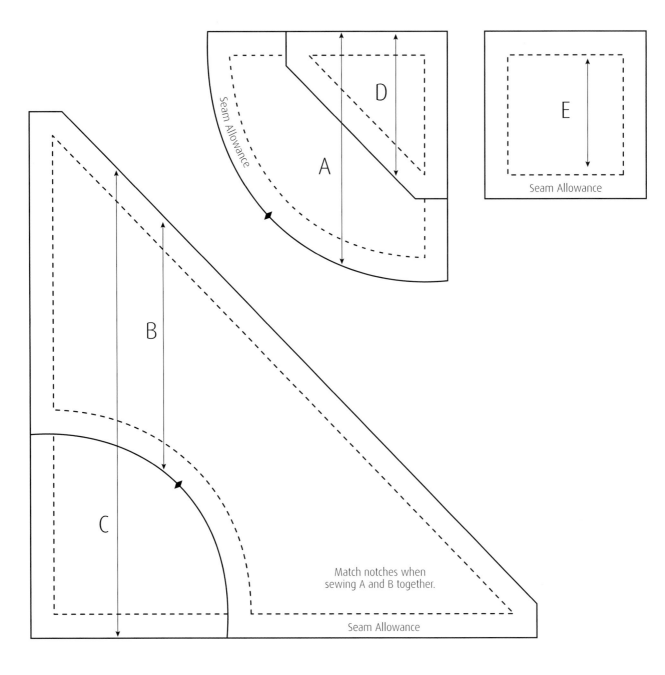

Seam Allowance

A

D

E

Seam Allowance

B

C

Match notches when
sewing A and B together.

Seam Allowance

ROTARY CUTTING

Measurements include ¼" seam allowance. Align arrows with lengthwise or crosswise grain of fabric.

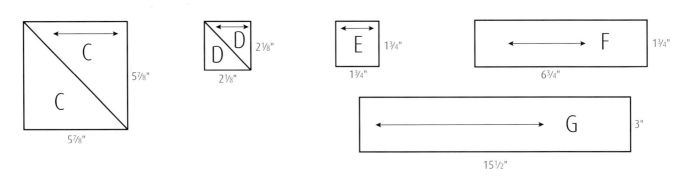

C

C

5⅞"

5⅞"

D

D

2⅛"

2⅛"

E

1¾"

1¾"

F

6¾"

1¾"

G

15½"

3"

Colorado Log Cabin

JUDY MARTIN

Well-known quilt designer and author Judy Martin, of Grinnell, Iowa, has created a Log Cabin with a difference: stars are formed where the blocks meet. No matter what Log Cabin setting arrangement you choose, the stars appear, creating a lovely secondary pattern. The sewing is no harder than that for a Lemoyne Star—easy enough for a careful beginner. But with all of its fascinating possibilities, Colorado Log Cabin should keep the more-experienced quiltmaker interested, as well.

Made by Judy Martin.

Materials and Cutting

BLOCK SIZE: 12" × 12"

QUILT SIZE: 76" × 100"

◆ Requirements are based on 42" fabric width.

◆ Borders include 2" extra length plus seam allowances. Measure your top and cut to size.

◆ Read all instructions before cutting.

MATERIALS	YARDS	CUTTING
Dark Gold Print	1	48 A patches, 192 H patches
Medium Gold Print	⅞	192 H patches
Purple Stripe	3	
borders		2 at 2½" × 102½"
		2 at 2½" × 78½"
Brown Print	¾	
binding		9 strips 2½" × 42"
Dark Print Scraps	4	48 B patches, 48 C patches, 48 D patches, 48 E patches,
		48 F patches, 48 G patches, 96 I patches
Light Print Scraps	3½	48 A patches, 48 B patches, 48 C patches, 48 D patches,
		48 E patches, 48 F patches, 96 I patches
Backing	6⅛	2 panels 41" × 104"
Batting		80" × 104"

tips

Sort scraps into lights and darks, but be sure to include a few medium shades for variety. Add interest by using more than one color (this quilt has brown, green, and purple) in both the lights and the darks.

Like any other Log Cabin design, this quilt has many setting options. The arrangement shown is called Barn Raising. Other possibilities include diagonal bands of light and dark (Straight Furrows) and alternating crosses of light and dark (Sunshine and Shadows).

Getting Started

Wash and press fabrics. Cut the patches and other pieces as listed in the materials and cutting box. Refer to pages 104–107 for Quilting Basics.

Making the Blocks

1 Join the patches in alphabetical order from A–G, spiraling clockwise from the block center and referring to the block color and block piecing diagrams.

2 Join a dark gold H patch to one end of an I patch. Join a light gold H patch to the opposite end of the I patch. Repeat to make 3 additional H/I/H pieces, being careful to always place the dark gold H patch on the same end of the I patch.

3 Attach 1 H/I/H piece to each side of the block center, mitering the corners. Refer to the mitered corner borders section of Quilting Basics on pages 104–105.

4 Make 48 blocks.

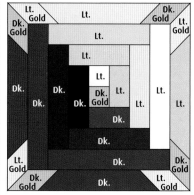

Block Colors

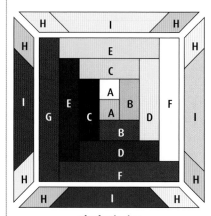

**Block Piecing
Make 48.**

Assembling the Quilt Top

1. Arrange the blocks in 8 rows of 6 blocks each. Turn the blocks so that the light/dark pattern matches the color photo of the quilt on page 33, or experiment with the block placement to create an individual look.

2. Join 6 blocks into a row, being careful to keep blocks turned according to design plan established in Step 1.

3. Make 8 rows.

4. Join the rows.

5. Sew the borders to the sides of the quilt, referring to the mitered corner borders section of Quilting Basics on pages 104–105. Sew the borders to the top and bottom of the quilt. Press the seam allowances toward the borders.

6. Miter the corners.

Quilting and Finishing

1. Layer and baste the quilt backing, batting, and top.

2. Quilt in-the-ditch between patches, or outline quilt ¼" from seamlines. Quilt in-the-ditch along border seamlines.

3. Trim quilt backing and batting even with the quilt top.

4. Join 2½"-wide strips diagonally to make the binding. Bind the quilt.

Align arrows with lengthwise or crosswise grain of fabric.

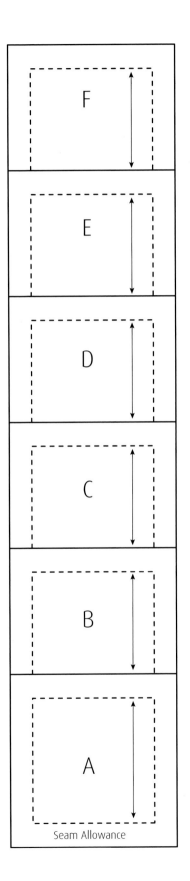

Seam Allowance

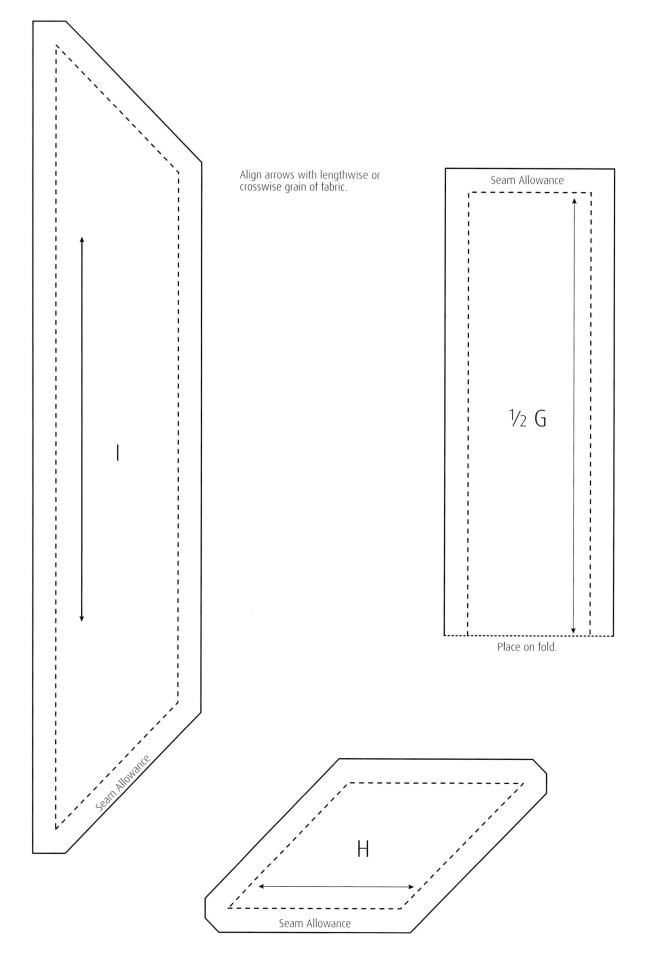

Align arrows with lengthwise or crosswise grain of fabric.

I

Seam Allowance

Seam Allowance

½ G

Place on fold.

H

Seam Allowance

Floral Trails Folk Art

KATHLEEN McCRADY

An 1860 quilt made in Pennsylvania, and owned by the Museum Quilts Gallery in London, was the inspiration for this quilt. Kathleen McCrady of Austin, Texas, writes, "I drafted the pieced block with slight modifications from the original, and paper-cut the appliqué motif for the alternate blocks. It is hand pieced and hand appliquéd." The original quilt has an appliqué border, but this designer chose to use the large blue floral print and added triple diagonal lines for the quilting.

Made by Kathleen McCrady.

Materials and Cutting

BLOCK SIZE: 12" × 12"

QUILT SIZE: 93½" × 93½"

◆ Requirements are based on 42" fabric width.

◆ Borders and sashes are the exact length required plus seam allowances.

◆ Read all instructions before cutting.

MATERIALS	YARDS	CUTTING
Cream Print	2½	9 motifs, 12 half motifs, 4 quarter motifs, 64 C patches,
		64 D patches, 192 F patches, 192 Fr patches
Light Gray Print	2¼	9 J patches, 12 K patches, 4 L patches
Red Print	2⅜ [*½]	52 hearts, 9 I patches
middle borders (side)		2 at 1¼" × 78"
middle borders (top/bottom)		2 at 1¼" × 76½"
Blue Print	2⅞ [*1½]	
inner borders (side)		2 at 1" × 76½"
inner borders (top/bottom)		2 at 1" × 75½"
sashes		2 at 1¾" × 94½"
sashes		2 at 1¾" × 68"
sashes		2 at 1¾" × 41½"
sashes		2 at 1¾" × 15"
short sashes		32 at 1¾" × 12½"
Blue Floral Print	3½	
outer borders (side)		2 at 8½" × 94"
outer borders (top/bottom)		2 at 8½" × 78"
binding		10 strips 2½" × 42"
Large-Scale Floral	1⅛	64 G patches
Light/Medium Scraps	1½	16 A patches, 128 B patches, 192 E patches
Backing	8⅝	3 panels 33" × 98"
Batting		98" × 98"

*Yardage given in [ ] is for borders and sashes cut crosswise and pieced.

⭐ *tips* Refer to the quilt photo for ideas for value placement in the pieced blocks. Note that some of the blocks have medium or dark squares (G patches) in the corners, while others have lighter squares.

Getting Started

Wash and press fabrics. Cut the patches and other pieces as listed in the materials and cutting box. Refer to pages 104–107 for Quilting Basics.

Making the Blocks

1 Join A, B, C, D, E, F, Fr, and G patches to make a block, referring to Block Piecing.

2 Make 16 blocks.

3 Fold an 11" × 11" square of freezer paper diagonally and trace the appliqué motif (H patch) on it, including the 4 heart shapes.

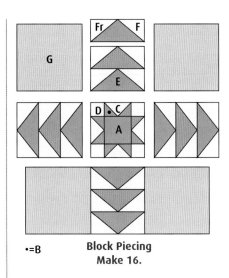

•=B

Block Piecing
Make 16.

4 Cut out the motif along the traced lines and cut out the hearts, but not the center 4-pointed star (I patch).

5 Iron the freezer-paper template to the right side of the cream fabric. Lightly mark the fabric around the freezer paper, including the edges of the freezer-paper hearts. Do not cut the cream fabric at this time. Remove the freezer paper.

6 Place the right side of a 2³⁄₄" × 2³⁄₄" square of red fabric against the wrong side of the cream fabric, centering underneath a drawn heart. Baste the red square to the cream fabric approximately ¼" outside the marked heart. From the right side, trim inside the marked heart, using sharp scissors and leaving a ³⁄₁₆" or less turn-under allowance. Needle-turn the cream fabric along the marked line and appliqué the heart-shaped opening to the red fabric. On the wrong side, trim away the excess red fabric ³⁄₁₆" beyond the appliqué stitching line and remove the basting.

7 Repeat for remaining 3 hearts.

8 Lightly crease vertical and horizontal lines on the J patches. Center the cream motif (H) on the J patch and baste inside the marked lines around the outer edge. Cut away only a short section of the motif at a time to prevent fraying, leaving a ³⁄₁₆" turn-under allowance. Needle-turn and appliqué the motif to the background along the marked line, using matching thread. Clip inside curves as needed. Continue to cut and stitch around the entire motif. On the wrong side, trim away the background fabric underneath the motif ³⁄₁₆" beyond the appliqué stitching line and remove the basting.

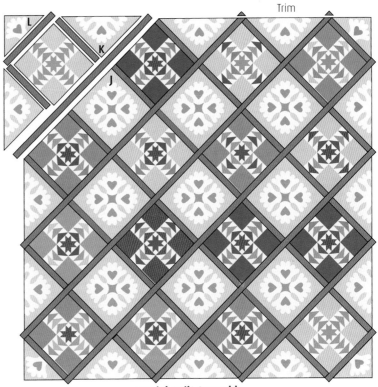

Partial Quilt Assembly

9 Cut the 4-pointed star center (I patch) from freezer paper. Iron the freezer-paper template to the right side of the red fabric. Mark the sewing line around the paper and trim fabric ³⁄₁₆" or less beyond the line. Remove the freezer paper. Turn under edges and appliqué the I patch to the cream motif, aligning the points with the creased lines of the background.

10 Repeat Steps 3–9 to make 9 appliquéd blocks.

11 Repeat Steps 3–9 to make 12 half- and 4 quarter-blocks. Appliqué the half-motifs on the 12 K patches and the quarter-motifs on the 4 L patches. The designer included the red heart in only one place on the half-blocks. The half hearts that are at the edges of the K patches are turned and stitched to the background with no red fabric added underneath the opening.

Assembling the Quilt Top

1 Arrange the blocks, the short sashes, and the K and L patches in diagonal rows on a large, flat surface, referring to Partial Quilt Assembly.

2 Join the blocks and short sashes to make rows.

3 Join the rows, sewing the appropriate length long sash between them.

4 Trim the sashes even with the quilt-top edges.

5 Sew the inner border to the top and bottom of the quilt top, then to the sides.

6 Sew the middle border to the top and bottom of the quilt top, then to the sides.

7 Sew the outer border to the top and bottom of the quilt top, then to the sides. Press the seam allowances toward the borders.

Quilting and Finishing

1 Layer and baste the quilt backing, batting, and top.

2 Quilt in-the-ditch around the block patches and along the sashes and borders. Quilt ¼" inside the appliqué motifs and ½" away from the edge of the cream motifs. Quilt along the printed design in the floral border, or quilt triple diagonal lines in the border.

3 Trim quilt backing and batting even with the quilt top.

4 Join 2½"-wide strips diagonally to make the binding. Bind the quilt.

ROTARY CUTTING
Measurements include ¼" seam allowance. Align arrows with lengthwise or crosswise grain of fabric.

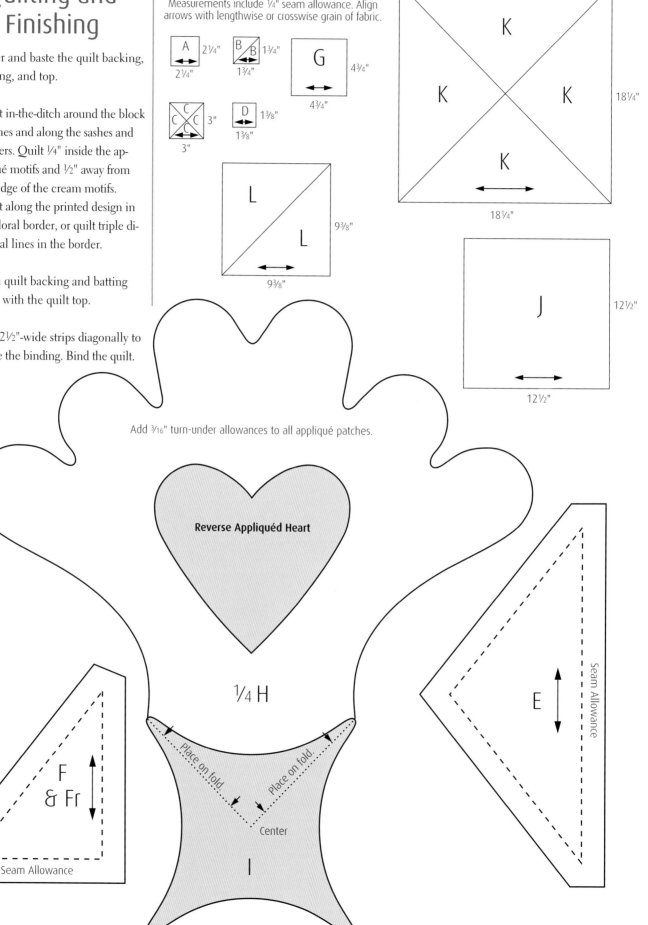

A 2¼"
2¼"

B/B 1¾"
1¾"

G 4¾"
4¾"

C/C/C 3"
3"

D 1⅜"
1⅜"

K K K K K
18¼"
18¼"

L L
9⅜"
9⅜"

J
12½"
12½"

Add ³⁄₁₆" turn-under allowances to all appliqué patches.

Reverse Appliquéd Heart

¼ H

Place on fold   Place on fold
Center
I

F & Fr
Seam Allowance

E
Seam Allowance

Snail's Trail

YOKO KIKUCHI AND YAEKO SASAJIMA

An old pattern gets a new twist with this Snail's Trail made by these quiltmakers from Japan. The pattern is traditionally colored with two opposite "arms" or swirls in medium/dark fabrics and the other two swirls in light fabrics. The blocks are generally set with alternating plain blocks that match the darker swirls. In Yoko's variation, the blocks are colored with one or two light swirls, then set with narrow sashing and setting squares. Visually, the light patches join at the setting squares to form large pinwheels. The small block size allows the use of very small scraps of fabric, making this a perfect carry-along pattern.

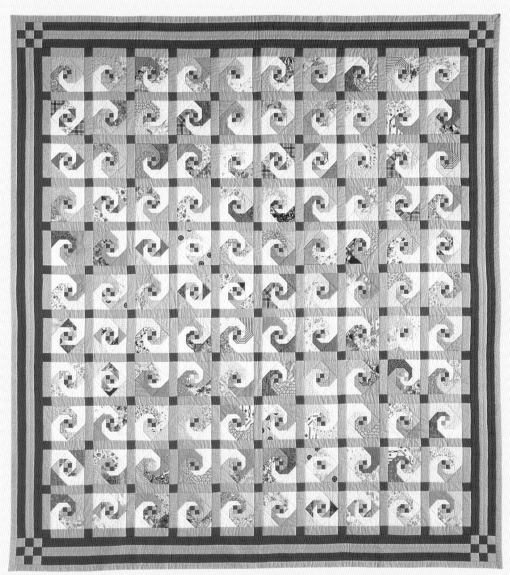

Designed by Yoko Kikuchi. Made by Yaeko Sasajima.

Materials and Cutting

BLOCK SIZE: 6" × 6"

QUILT SIZE: 88½" × 96"

◆ Requirements are based on 42" fabric width.

◆ Outer borders include 2" extra length plus seam allowances. Measure your top and cut to size.

◆ Read all instructions before cutting.

MATERIALS	YARDS	CUTTING
White Solid	1⅝	110 B patches, 110 C patches, 110 D patches, 110 E patches
Gray Solid	2½	220 A patches, 148 G patches
inner borders (sides)		2 at 2" × 84½"
outer borders (sides)		2 at 2" × 84½"
inner borders (top/bottom)		2 at 2" × 77"
outer borders (top/bottom)		2 at 2" × 77"
Peach Solid	4½	220 A patches, 20 G patches
sashing		241 F patches
middle borders (sides)		2 at 2" × 84½"
middle borders (top/bottom)		2 at 2" × 77"
outermost borders (sides)		2 at 2" × 98½"
outermost borders (top/bottom)		2 at 2" × 91"
binding		10 strips 1½" × 42"
Print Scraps	5	330 B patches, 330 C patches, 330 D patches, 330 E patches
Backing	8⅛	3 panels 34" × 92½"
Batting		92½" × 100"

tips

The designer planned 2 different color variations for the blocks. Variation 1 uses 3 medium/medium light print fabrics and a solid white for the 4 swirls of the Snail's Trail. Variation 2 uses 2 medium prints, 1 light print, and a solid white. The quilt shown uses 60 Variation 1 blocks and 50 Variation 2 blocks. This scheme or any combination of it can be followed. Just be sure that each block has at least 1 light swirl.

In true quilter tradition, a few of the Four-Patch units in the block centers were made with slightly different fabrics.

For patches A, B, C, D, E, and G you can either rotary cut the squares, then cut them diagonally in half as indicated, or you can make templates. Both are given on page 44.

Getting Started

Wash and press fabrics. Cut the patches and other pieces as listed in the materials and cutting box. Refer to pages 104–107 for Quilting Basics.

Making the Blocks

1 Join 2 peach solid and 2 gray solid A patches to make a Four-Patch unit.

2 Make 110 Four-Patch units.

3 Join B, C, D, and E patches to a Four-Patch unit to make a block.

4 Make 60 blocks using Variation 1 and 50 blocks using Variation 2, for a total of 110 blocks.

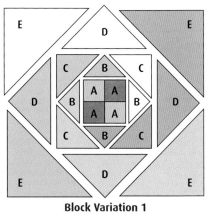

Block Variation 1
Make 60.

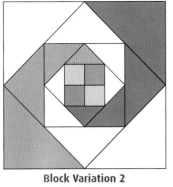

Block Variation 2
Make 50.

5 Join 4 gray solid G patches and 5 peach solid G patches to make a corner unit, referring to Corner Unit Piecing.

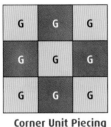

Corner Unit Piecing
Make 4.

6 Make 4 corner units.

Assembling the Quilt Top

1 Arrange the blocks, F patches, and G patches on a large, flat surface. Turn some blocks so that the light/white swirls come together around the G patches to form the large, white pinwheels.

2 Join 10 blocks and 11 sashing pieces for each block row, beginning with a sashing piece and alternating sashing pieces and blocks. Press seam allowances toward sashing.

3 Make 11 block rows.

4 Join 10 sashing pieces and 11 G patches to make a sashing row, beginning with a G patch and alternating G patches and sashing pieces. Press seam allowances toward sashing.

5 Make 12 sashing rows.

6 Join block rows and sashing rows, beginning with a sashing row and alternating sashing rows and block rows. Press seam allowances in one direction.

7 Sew an inner gray side border, a middle peach side border, and an outer gray side border together to make a side border. Press the seam allowances toward the dark fabric.

8 Make 2 side borders.

9 Sew an inner gray top/bottom border, a middle peach top/bottom border, and an outer gray top/bottom border together to make a top/bottom border. Press the seam allowances toward the dark fabric.

10 Make 2 top/bottom borders.

11 Sew the borders to the sides of quilt, referring to the butted borders section of Quilting Basics on page 104. Sew a corner unit to each end of the top/bottom borders. Sew the borders to the top and bottom, matching seams at the corners. Press the seam allowances toward the borders.

Note: The quiltmaker used wide binding to form the final peach border. We give directions for a 1½"-wide outer peach border and a traditional binding.

12 Sew the outermost peach borders to the sides of the quilt, referring to the mitered corner borders section of Quilting Basics on pages 104–105. Sew the outermost peach borders to the top and bottom of the quilt. Press the seam allowances toward the dark fabric.

13 Miter the corners.

Quilting and Finishing

1 Layer and baste the quilt backing, batting, and top.

2 Quilt in-the-ditch around patches A–D. Quilt ¼" from seamlines of the E patches and the borders.

3 Trim quilt backing and batting even with the quilt top.

4 Join 1½"-wide strips diagonally to make the binding. Bind the quilt.

Align arrows with lengthwise or crosswise grain of fabric.

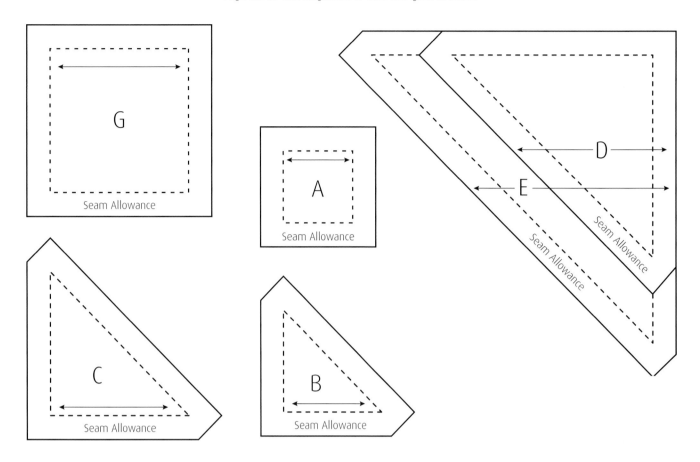

ROTARY CUTTING

Measurements include ¼" seam allowance. Align arrows with lengthwise or crosswise grain of fabric.

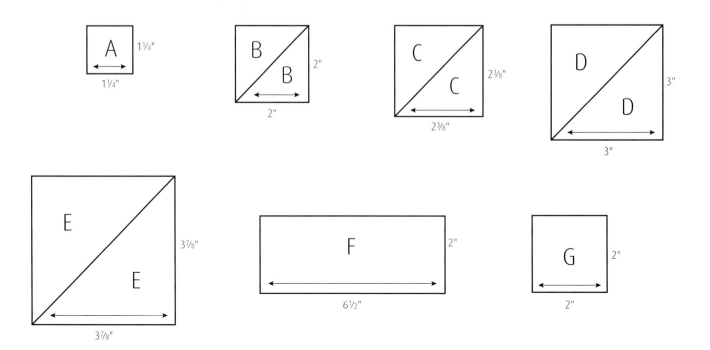

Twilight Flock

Stitch a gaggle of geese to make this delightful quilt. The pattern for Twilight Flock was adapted from a quilt that is in the collection of Shelburne Museum, in Vermont. The blocks for this quilt were enlarged from 9" to 12" to make the pieces easier to handle for less-experienced quiltmakers. The larger size also resulted in a bed-size quilt suitable for a queen coverlet.

Maker unknown

Materials and Cutting

BLOCK SIZE: 12" × 12"

QUILT SIZE: 72" × 84"

◆ Requirements are based on 42" fabric width.

◆ Read all instructions before cutting.

MATERIALS	YARDS	CUTTING
Black Solid	4	1,008 B patches
binding		8 strips 2½" × 42"
Striped Scraps	2½	336 C patches
Print Scraps	2⅝	504 A patches
Backing	5¼	2 panels 38½" × 88"
Batting		76" × 88"

✦ tips

For the most part, the 3 geese in each quarter of a block are all cut from the same fabric. The quiltmaker used stripes for many of the C patches, and chose black scraps for the background B patches. For those not fond of black, the B patches can be cut from any dark fabric.

For patches A and B you can either rotary cut the squares, then cut as indicated, or you can make triangle templates. Both are given on page 48.

Getting Started

Wash and press fabrics. Cut the patches and other pieces as listed in the materials and cutting box. Refer to pages 104–107 for Quilting Basics.

Making the Blocks

1 Join 1 A patch and 2 B patches to make a flying-geese unit. For speedy construction, refer to the chain piecing instructions on the next page.

**Flying-Geese Unit
Make 504.**

2 Make 504 flying-geese units.

3 Join 3 flying-geese units and sew C patches to each side, referring to Block Piecing, to make a quarter block.

4 Make 168 quarter blocks.

5 Sew 4 quarter blocks together to make a block, paying particular attention to the direction of the geese.

6 Make 42 blocks.

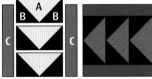

**Block Piecing
Make 42.**

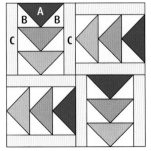

Alternate Color Variation

Assembling the Quilt Top

1 Arrange the blocks on a flat surface or design wall in 7 rows of 6 blocks each until satisfied with color placement.

2 Sew the blocks in rows.

3 Join the rows. Press the seam allowances in one direction.

Quilting and Finishing

1 Layer and baste the quilt backing, batting, and top.

2 Quilt in-the-ditch along major seamlines and ¼" away from the edges of all A patches.

3 Trim quilt backing and batting even with the quilt top.

4 Join 2½"-wide strips diagonally to make the binding. Bind the quilt.

CHAIN PIECING

1 Machine sew a B patch to an A patch to make an A-B unit. Sew off the edge of the unit for several stitches, forming a chain. Without lifting the needle or cutting the threads, sew another A-B unit and, again, make a chain of stitches at the end.

2 Continue sewing A-B units in this manner, leaving them connected by the chains and letting them pile up on the table or floor behind your sewing machine.

3 Cut the chain of units into manageable sections of 10–12 units for pressing.

4 Press seam allowances toward the B patches.

5 Cut apart all the units.

6 Sew the remaining B patches to the A-B units to complete the flying-geese units.

7 Continue in this manner to chain piece the flying-geese units, the C patches, and the quarter blocks.

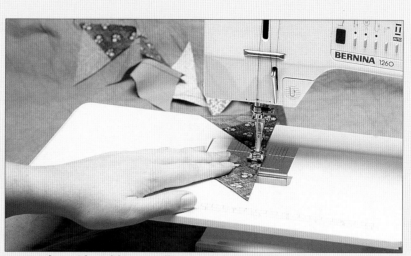

Sew patches without lifting needle or cutting threads.

Sew a chain of patches.

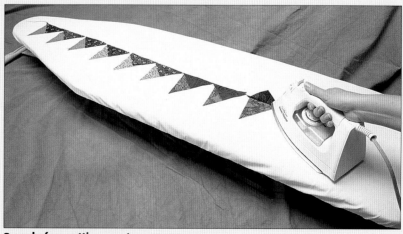

Press before cutting apart.

ROTARY CUTTING

Measurements include ¼" seam allowance. Align arrows with lengthwise or crosswise grain of fabric.

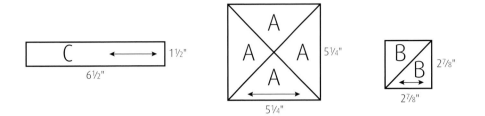

Align arrows with lengthwise or crosswise grain of fabric.

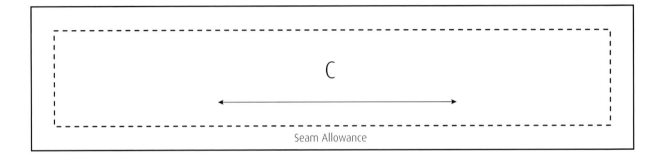

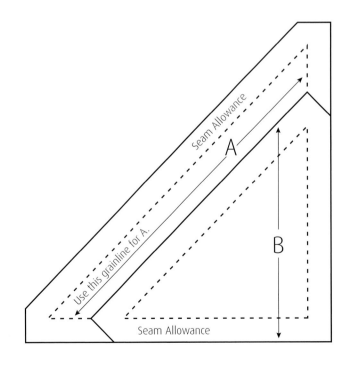

Techny Chimes

NANCY PEARSON

The design for Techny Chimes was inspired by a strain of day lilies developed by Brother Charles at a missionary society located not far from the designer's hometown of Morton Grove, Illinois. The flower is named for Techny, the mother house for the society. Nancy designed the appliqué to honor the work of Brother Charles. Techny Chimes was one of the first three quilts she entered in the International Quilt Festival, in Houston, in 1984. The quilt, which won five ribbons, was featured on the cover of Quilter's Newsletter Magazine *in April 1985. It now resides in the women's wing of Rush-Presbyterian-St. Luke's Medical Center in Chicago.*

Made by Nancy Pearson.

Materials and Cutting

QUILT SIZE: 59¼" × 59¼"

◆ Requirements are based on 42" fabric width.

◆ Pieced borders are the exact length required plus seam allowances.

◆ Strip borders include 2½" extra length plus seam allowances. Measure your top and cut to size.

◆ Read all instructions before cutting.

MATERIALS	YARDS	CUTTING
Cream Solid	1	1 A patch, 288 D patches
White Solid	2	1 F patch
middle borders		4 at 6½" × 47½"
Sage Green Print	2 [*⅝]	89 laurel leaves
outer borders		4 at 1⅜" × 62¼"
Sage Green Stripe	1¾	
outer borders		4 at ⅞" × 60½"
outer middle borders		4 at ⅞" × 48¼"
inner middle borders		4 at ⅞" × 35½"
inner borders		4 at ⅞" × 27¼"
Dark Green Solid	1¼	
bias vines		18 yards bias ⅞" wide
binding		6 strips 2½" × 42"
Light Blue Solid	¼	40 C patches, 24 D patches
Medium Blue Solid	¼	40 C patches, 24 D patches
Light Gray Solid	⅜	208 D patches
Medium Gray Solid	⅝	48 C patches, 96 D patches, 48 E patches
Light Pink Solid	⅜	28 B patches, 48 D patches, 24 E patches
Pink Solid	⅜	28 B patches, 48 D patches, 24 E patches
Peach Solid	1¾ [*¾]	
outer borders		4 at 1⅜" × 59¾"
outer middle borders		4 at 1⅜" × 50"
inner middle borders		4 at 1⅜" × 34¾"
inner borders		4 at 1⅜" × 29"
Green Scraps	¾	46 leaves, 28 bases for flowers, 33 strawberry tops
Pink/Red Scraps	¾	28 flowers, 33 strawberries, 26 cherries
Backing	3¾	2 panels 32" × 64"
Batting		63¼" × 63¼"

*Yardage given in [ ] is for borders cut crosswise and pieced.

Supplies: Sage-colored embroidery floss

✦tips The border appliqué pattern must be enlarged 400%. Depending on the copy machine used, the pattern may have to be enlarged by 200%; then enlarge the copy by 200% to total 400%.

Getting Started

Wash and press fabrics. Cut the patches and other pieces as listed in the materials and cutting box. Refer to pages 104–107 for Quilting Basics.

Making the Blocks

1 Work from the center of the F patch and use a compass or a pencil and string to draw a circle with an 8¼" radius on the square.

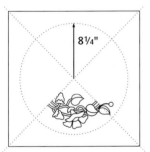

8¼"

Center Appliqué Placement

2 Fold the square in quarters diagonally and finger-press creases along the folds to mark the location of appliqué placement. Place the quarter center appliqué pattern beneath the square, aligning the creases with the dotted lines of the pattern. Trace the quarter design, referring to Center Appliqué Placement. Rotate the pattern, align, and trace again. Repeat to complete the design.

3 To make the vine and stems, fold the green bias strip in half lengthwise with the wrong sides of the fabric together. Sew ¼" in from the raw edges. Trim close to the stitching. Fold the seam allowances under and press, hiding the stitching line underneath.

Make ¼" finished bias vines and stems.

4 Cut lengths of bias vine as needed, position, pin, and blindstitch in place.

5 Appliqué the flowers, leaves, strawberries, and cherries, working from the bottommost patches toward the top patches.

6 Cut the white circle from the F patch leaving a ³⁄₁₆" turn-under allowance beyond the marked line.

7 Fold the A patch diagonally into quarters and finger-press creases along the folds. Fold again horizontally and vertically, finger-pressing creases along the folds.

8 Center the white circle on the A patch, matching the diagonal creases. Appliqué the F patch in place.

9 Work from the center of the A patch and use a compass or a pencil and string to draw a circle with a 10" radius on the patch.

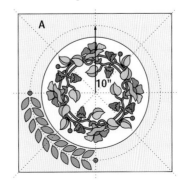

A

10"

Laurel Leaf Placement

10 Make the stem for the laurel leaves by embroidering the marked circle with an outline stitch. Use 3 strands of embroidery floss for the embroidery. Place the cherries on the horizontal and vertical centers of the circle. Arrange the laurel leaves as shown in the quilt photo on page 49, noting the change in direction of the leaves.

11 Appliqué the leaves and cherries to complete the center block. Set aside.

12 Join B, C, and D patches to make inner border units, referring to Inner Border Piecing for patch color placement.

B

Inner Border Piecing Unit 1 Make 28.

D
C

Inner Border Piecing Unit 2 Make 24.

D
D

Inner Border Piecing Unit 3 Make 4.

13 Make 28 of unit 1, 24 of unit 2, and 4 of unit 3.

14 Join C, D, and E patches to make outer border units, referring to Outer Border Piecing for patch color placement.

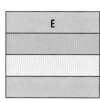

**Outer Border Piecing
Unit 4
Make 24.**

**Outer Border Piecing
Unit 5
Make 8.**

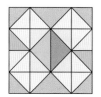

**Outer Border Piecing
Unit 6
Make 8.**

**Outer Border Piecing
Unit 7
Make 4.**

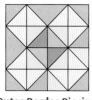

**Outer Border Piecing
Unit 8
Make 4.**

15 Make 24 of unit 4, 8 of unit 5, 8 of unit 6, 4 of unit 7, and 4 of unit 8. Set aside.

Assembling the Quilt Top

1 Match the center of a green stripe inner border and a peach inner border. Join the borders. Repeat for the remaining inner borders.

2 Sew assembled inner borders to the sides of the center block, starting and stopping stitching ¼" from each edge. Sew inner borders to the top and bottom of the center block.

3 Miter the corners, referring to Quilting Basics on page 104–107.

4 Join 7 of unit 1 and 6 of unit 2 to make an inner pieced border, beginning with a unit 1, alternating the units, and noting the orientation of the B and C patches. Refer to Quilt Assembly. Repeat for the remaining inner pieced borders.

5 Sew inner pieced borders to the sides of the quilt. Add a unit 3 to each end of the remaining inner pieced borders and sew borders to the top and bottom of the quilt.

6 Matching the centers, join middle border strips in the following order: inner middle peach, inner middle green stripe, white, outer middle green stripe, and outer middle peach. Repeat for the remaining middle borders.

7 Sew assembled middle borders to the sides of the quilt, starting and stopping stitching ¼" from each edge. Sew middle borders to the top and bottom of the quilt.

8 Miter the corners.

9 Join 6 of unit 4, 2 of unit 5, 2 of unit 6, and 1 of unit 7, referring to Quilt Assembly for placement and noting

Quilt Assembly

the orientation of the pink D patches. Repeat for the remaining outer pieced borders.

10 Sew outer pieced borders to the sides of the quilt. Add a unit 8 to each end of the remaining outer pieced borders, orienting the units as shown in Quilt Assembly. Sew outer pieced borders to the top and bottom of the quilt.

11 Matching the centers, join outer border strips in the following order: peach, green stripe, and green print. Repeat for the remaining outer borders.

12 Sew assembled outer borders to the sides of the quilt, starting and stopping stitching ¼" from each edge. Sew outer borders to the top and bottom.

13 Miter the corners.

14 Press the seam allowances toward the borders.

15 Enlarge the border appliqué placement pattern 400%.

16 Position the vines, stems, and appliqué patches along the white border, referring to appliqué placement. Note that each corner of the quilt has a different floral arrangement. Feel free to create your own arrangement.

17 Blindstitch the patches and embroider the stems for the cherries.

Quilting and Finishing

1 Mark the floral quilting motif in the center of the white circle.

2 Layer and baste the quilt backing, batting, and top.

3 Quilt in-the-ditch around the pieced patches and borders. Quilt the marked floral motif and ⅛" from the edge of the appliqué. Quilt a grid of 1" hanging squares in the cream

background. The designer quilted vines and leaves in the outer pieced border, using the appliqué leaves as a pattern.

4 Trim quilt backing and batting even with the quilt top.

5 Join 2½"-wide strips diagonally to make the binding. Bind the quilt.

ROTARY CUTTING

Measurements include ¼" seam allowance. Align arrows with lengthwise or crosswise grain of fabric.

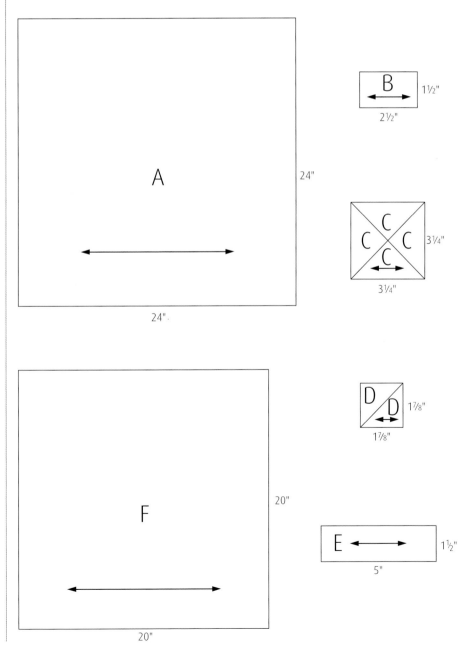

Center

Border Appliqué Placement
Enlarge 400%.

Center

Add ³⁄₁₆" turn-under
allowance for traditional appliqué.

¼ **Center Appliqué Motif**

Add ³⁄₁₆"
turn-under
allowance for
traditional
appliqué.

Laurel Leaf

↑ Place on fold. ↑

½ **Floral Quilting**

Fire Lily

ORIGINAL DESIGN BY KAORI KASUYA, ADAPTED BY BARBARA WILLIAMS

When Barbara Williams of St. Petersburg, Florida, was called on to chair the raffle committee of the Suncoast Quilting Circle, little did she know that she would be adapting and redrafting the dramatic and stunning quilt MOMI, made by Kaori Kasuya of Japan, which had been featured on the cover of Quilter's Newsletter Magazine. *She simplified the diamond patches Kaori used into half-square triangles and her guild members began to sew.*

Made by Barbara Williams and others. Quilted by Dea Crandall.

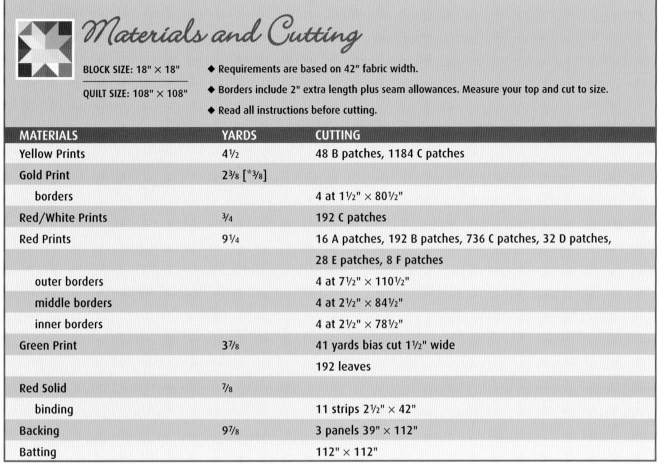

Materials and Cutting

BLOCK SIZE: 18" × 18"

QUILT SIZE: 108" × 108"

◆ Requirements are based on 42" fabric width.

◆ Borders include 2" extra length plus seam allowances. Measure your top and cut to size.

◆ Read all instructions before cutting.

MATERIALS	YARDS	CUTTING
Yellow Prints	4½	48 B patches, 1184 C patches
Gold Print	2⅜ [*⅜]	
borders		4 at 1½" × 80½"
Red/White Prints	¾	192 C patches
Red Prints	9¼	16 A patches, 192 B patches, 736 C patches, 32 D patches,
		28 E patches, 8 F patches
outer borders		4 at 7½" × 110½"
middle borders		4 at 2½" × 84½"
inner borders		4 at 2½" × 78½"
Green Print	3⅞	41 yards bias cut 1½" wide
		192 leaves
Red Solid	⅞	
binding		11 strips 2½" × 42"
Backing	9⅞	3 panels 39" × 112"
Batting		112" × 112"

*Yardage given in [ ] is for borders cut crosswise and pieced.

tips The red borders of the original quilt are made up of strips approximately 10" long, pieced end-to-end to get the length required. This method can be used, or a single strip can be cut to the length indicated for the borders. If cutting full-length borders, cut them first and then cut the patches from the remaining fabric.

Enlarge appliqué patterns as indicated.

Getting Started

Wash and press fabrics. Cut the patches and other pieces as listed in the materials and cutting box. Refer to pages 104–107 for Quilting Basics.

Making the Blocks

1 Join A, B, C, and D patches to make a Z block, referring to Block Z Piecing.

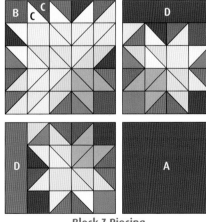

Block Z Piecing
Make 16.

2 Make 16 Z blocks.

3 Join B and C patches to make a border block, referring to Border Block Piecing.

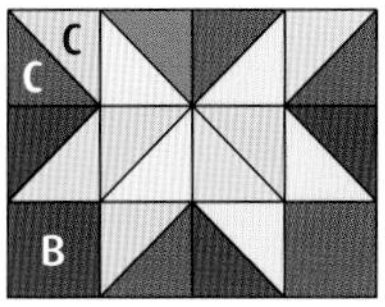

Border Block Piecing
Make 32.

4 Make 32 border blocks.

Assembling the Quilt Top

1 Join the Z blocks into 4 units of 4 blocks each, referring to Partial Quilt Assembly and Appliqué Placement and orienting the blocks as shown.

2 Make the bias vines.

3 Arrange the vines and leaves, using the enlarged block appliqué pattern as a placement guide and referring to the photo and Partial Quilt Assembly and Appliqué Placement.

4 Appliqué the vines and leaves in place. Turn under the ends of the vines and appliqué in place.

5 Piece the red border strips (if needed) to get the required border lengths.

6 Find the center of an inner red border and align it with the center of a gold border.

7 Join the borders.

8 Match the center of a middle red border with the center of a gold border.

9 Join the borders.

10 Join 8 border blocks and 7 E patches, beginning with a border block and alternating blocks and patches. Add an F patch to each end.

11 Center and sew this pieced border to the joined borders.

12 Center and sew the final red border to complete the border unit.

13 Repeat Steps 6–12 for the remaining border units.

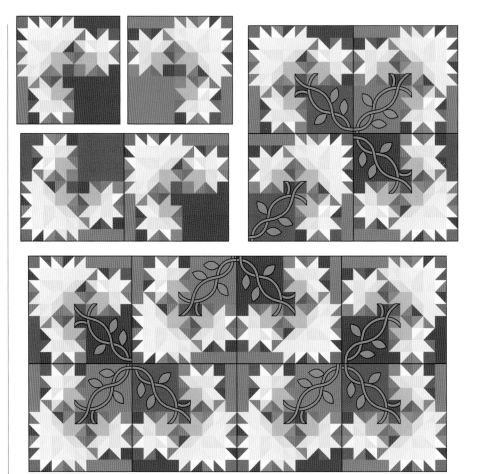

Partial Quilt Assembly and Appliqué Placement

Miter seam, then trim.

Border Assembly

14 Sew a border unit to one side of the quilt, starting and stopping stitching ¼" from the edges of the quilt top.

15 Repeat for the opposite side, the top, and the bottom. Press the seam allowances toward the borders.

16 Miter the corners, referring to the mitered corner borders section of Quilting Basics on pages 104–105.

17 Arrange the vines and leaves on the outer border, using the enlarged corner and border appliqué patterns as placement guides and referring to the photo and Corner and Border Appliqué Placement. Begin in a corner and mark the number of segments shown toward the center. Move to the opposite corner and repeat. Repeat for the remaining 3 sides of the quilt top. Complete the curves to join the stems. Note that the leaves and vines reverse direction in the border centers.

18 Appliqué the stems and leaves in place. Appliqué the vines in place. Turn under the ends of the vines and appliqué in place.

Quilting and Finishing

1 Mark quilting designs as desired. The quilter stipple quilted the red background and border fabric, and quilted arcs in the flowers.

2 Layer and baste the quilt backing, batting, and top.

3 Quilt the designs as marked.

4 Trim quilt backing and batting even with the quilt top.

5 Join 2½"-wide strips diagonally to make the binding. Bind the quilt.

Corner and Border Appliqué Placement

ROTARY CUTTING
Measurements include ¼" seam allowance.
Align arrows with lengthwise or crosswise grain of fabric.

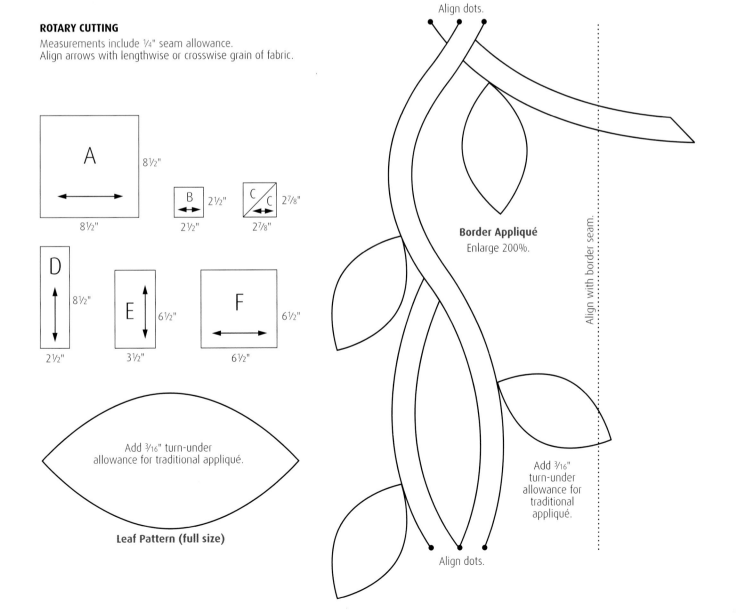

A 8½"
8½"

B 2½"
2½"

C / C 2⅞"
2⅞"

D 8½"
2½"

E 6½"
3½"

F 6½"
6½"

Add ³⁄₁₆" turn-under allowance for traditional appliqué.

Leaf Pattern (full size)

Align dots.

Border Appliqué
Enlarge 200%.

Align with border seam.

Add ³⁄₁₆" turn-under allowance for traditional appliqué.

Align dots.

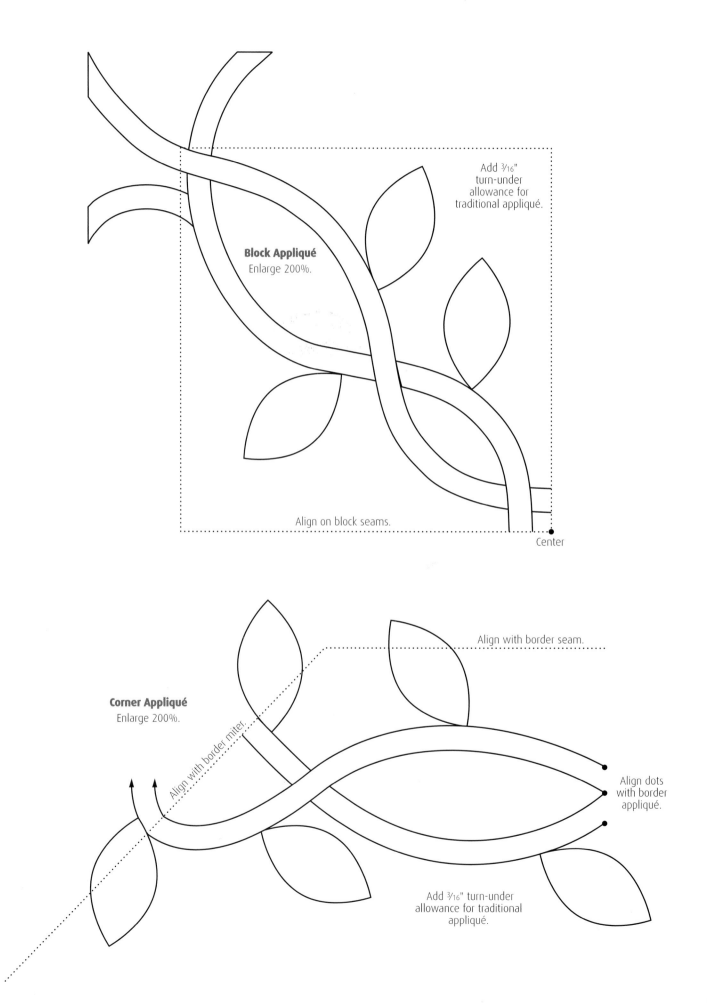

Add ³⁄₁₆"
turn-under
allowance for
traditional appliqué.

Block Appliqué
Enlarge 200%.

Align on block seams.

Center

Align with border seam.

Corner Appliqué
Enlarge 200%.

Align with border miter.

Align dots
with border
appliqué.

Add ³⁄₁₆" turn-under
allowance for traditional
appliqué.

Knutson Drive

Janine Holzman

Inspired to work with a tessellating pattern, Janine Holzman of Sitka, Alaska, chose the Double T design and made this quilt for her daughter, whose name begins with the letter T. The house border has been adapted for ease of piecing.

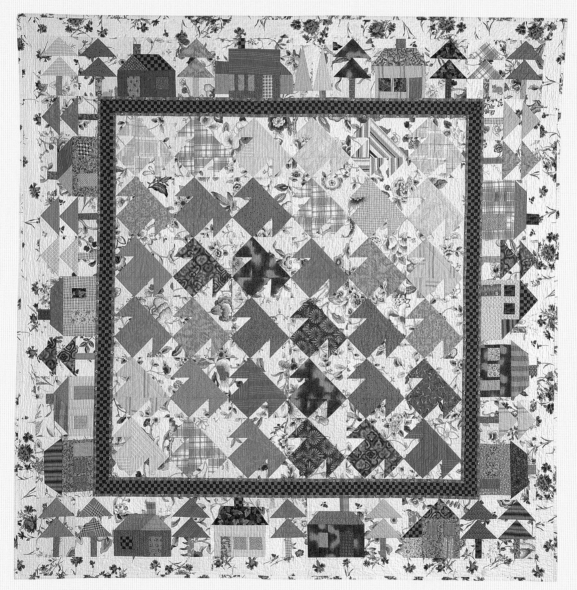

Made by Janine Holzman.

Materials and Cutting

BLOCK SIZE: 9" × 9", 6" × 9"

QUILT SIZE: 84" × 84"

◆ Requirements are based on 42" fabric width.

◆ Borders are the exact length required plus seam allowances.

◆ Read all instructions before cutting.

MATERIALS	YARDS	CUTTING
Cream Print	7	
outer borders		4 at 3½" × 84½"
binding		5 strips 2½" × 71"
		36 T1 patches, 180 T2 patches, background patches
		for houses and trees
Blue Scraps	3½	36 T1 patches, 180 T2 patches, patches for houses and trees
Pink Print	1⅞ [*½]	
inner borders		8 at 1" × 62½"
Pink Scraps	1	patches for houses and tree trunks
Blue/Black Check	1⅞ [*⅝]	
inner borders		4 at 2½" × 62½"
Backing	7¾	3 panels 30" × 88"
Batting		88" × 88"

*Yardage given in [ ] is for borders cut crosswise and pieced.

tips

When cutting the patches, note that some of the houses are reversed.

All of the units in the house border are divisible by 3". The house blocks finish 9" × 9". The tree blocks finish 6" × 9". If you prefer to design your own borders you can make and arrange houses and trees to fill the borders as desired. The pink house and conical trees at the top of the designer's quilt have been exchanged for other blocks.

Getting Started

Wash and press fabrics. Cut the patches and other pieces as listed in the materials and cutting box. Refer to pages 104–107 for Quilting Basics.

Making the Blocks

1 Join T1 and T2 patches to make a Double T block, referring to Double T Block Piecing.

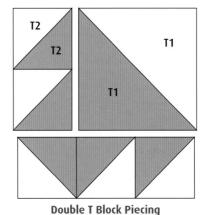

**Double T Block Piecing
Make 36.**

2 Make 36 Double T blocks.

3 Set aside.

4 Join R9, R29, T2, and T4 patches to make a tree block, referring to Tree Block Piecing.

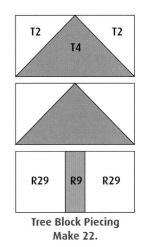

**Tree Block Piecing
Make 22.**

5 Make 22 tree blocks.

6 Join M2 or M2r, M3 or M3r, R1, R3, R10, R11, R12, R13, R14, S2, S3, S4, T2, T4, and T6 patches to make W blocks, referring to Block W Piecing.

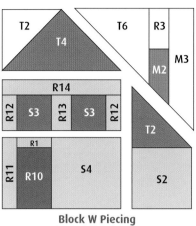

Block W Piecing
Make 2 and 1 reversed.

7 Make 2 W blocks and 1 reverse W block.

8 Join M4, M5, M5r, R2, R15, R16, R17, R18, R19, R20, S1, and S5 patches to make X blocks, referring to Block X Piecing.

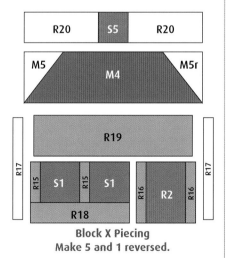

Block X Piecing
Make 5 and 1 reversed.

9 Make 5 X blocks and 1 reverse X block.

10 Join R6, R21, R22, R23, R24, R25, R26, R27, R28, and S1 patches to make Y blocks, referring to Block Y Piecing.

For the roof, draw a diagonal line on the wrong side of S1. Position S1, right sides together, at one end of R26. Stitch diagonally from corner to corner. Trim away the excess and press open. Repeat at other end.

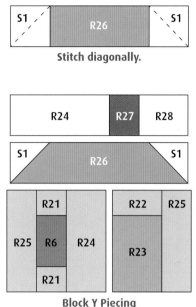

Stitch diagonally.

Block Y Piecing
Make 2 and 1 reversed.

11 Make 2 Y blocks and 1 reverse Y block.

12 Join M1 or M1r, R2, R3, R4, R5, R6, R7, R8, R21, S1, T3, and T5 patches to make Z blocks, referring to Block Z Piecing.

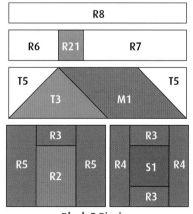

Block Z Piecing
Make 2 and 2 reversed.

13 Make 2 Z blocks and 2 reverse Z blocks.

Assembling the Quilt Top

1 Arrange the Double T blocks in 6 rows of 6 blocks each, orienting the blocks as shown in Quilt Assembly.

2 Join the rows.

3 Sew a blue check border strip between 2 pink border strips to make a border unit.

4 Make 4 border units.

5 Sew the border units to the sides of the quilt, referring to the mitered corner borders section of Quilting Basics on pages 104–105. Sew the border units to the top and bottom of the quilt. Press the seam allowances toward the borders.

6 Miter the corners.

7 Arrange the house and tree blocks to make 4 assembled borders, referring to Quilt Assembly for placement.

8 Join the blocks.

9 Sew the short assembled borders to the sides of the quilt. Sew the long assembled borders to the top and bottom of the quilt. Press the seam allowances toward the borders.

10 Sew the outer borders to the sides of the quilt, referring to the butted borders section of Quilting Basics on page 104. Sew the outer borders to the top and bottom of the quilt. Press the seam allowances toward the borders.

Quilt Assembly

Quilting and Finishing

1 Layer and baste the quilt backing, batting, and top.

2 Quilt in-the-ditch around the patches and borders. Echo quilt lines inside the Ts, and quilt straight lines through the houses and trees. Meander quilt the cream print background.

3 Trim quilt backing and batting even with the quilt top.

4 Join 2½"-wide strips diagonally to make the binding. Bind the quilt.

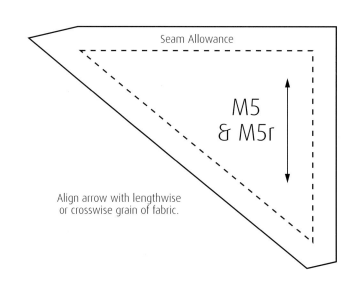

Seam Allowance

M5
& M5r

Align arrow with lengthwise or crosswise grain of fabric.

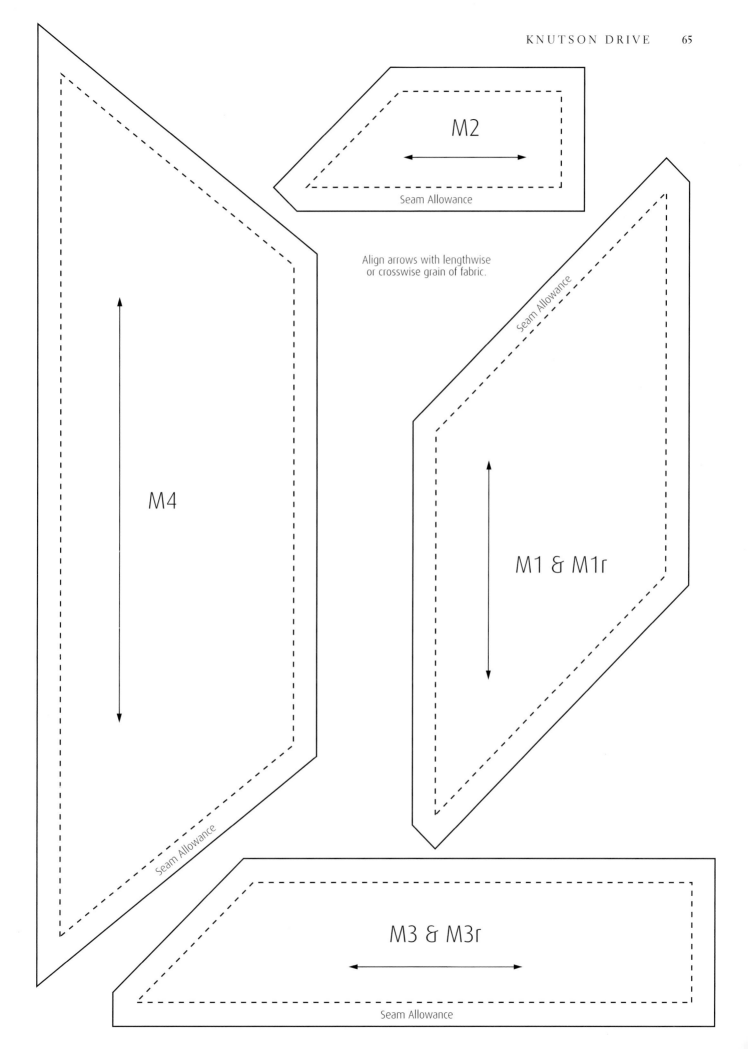

M2

Seam Allowance

Align arrows with lengthwise
or crosswise grain of fabric.

Seam Allowance

M4

M1 & M1r

Seam Allowance

M3 & M3r

Seam Allowance

ROTARY CUTTING

Measurements include ¼" seam allowance. Align arrows with lengthwise or crosswise grain of fabric.

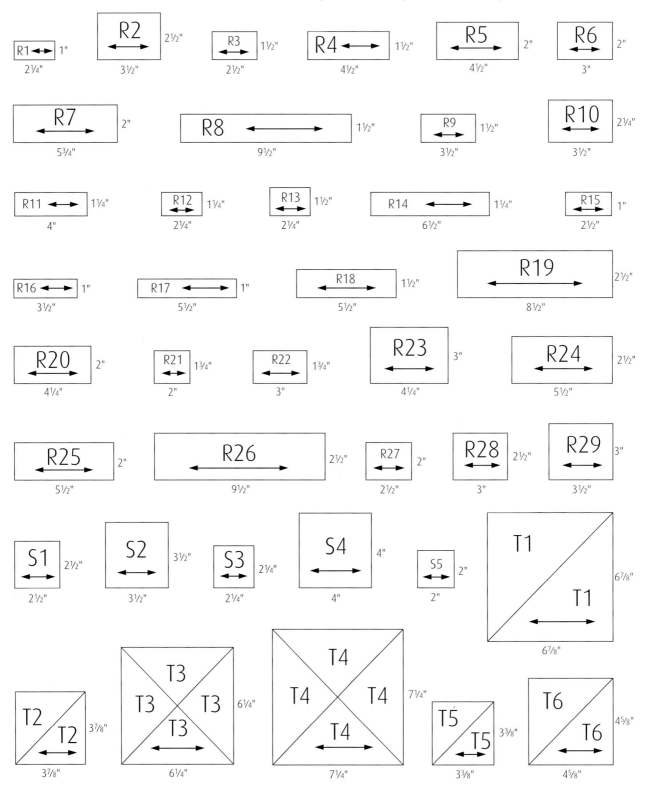

The Last Days

ROXI EPPLER HARDEGREE

It was an antique Crown of Thorns quilt that inspired Roxi Eppler Hardegree of Lubbock, Texas, to take on this quilt. The rich blend of red/orange and burgundy fabrics, complemented by the bright greens, creates a stunningly graphic design. Paper-foundation piecing techniques are used in the construction.

Made by Roxi Eppler Hardegree.

Materials and Cutting

BLOCK SIZE: 6" × 6", 9" × 9" ◆ Requirements are based on 42" fabric width.

QUILT SIZE: 59½" × 59½" ◆ Read all instructions before cutting. Cut foundation-piecing patches ¾" larger than pattern.

MATERIALS	YARDS	CUTTING
Red/Orange Scraps	2¾	24 A patches, 5 D patches, 32 flowers
foundation-piecing		paper-foundation patches for Crown of Thorns points (24 Blocks),
		paper-foundation patches for little star arcs (5 blocks)
Burgundy Prints	4½	16 B patches, 8 C patches, 4 F patches, 4 G patches, 4 Gr patches,
		4 H patches, paper-foundation patches for Crown of Thorns
		arcs (24 Blocks), paper-foundation patches for little star
		points (5 blocks)
Green Print	⅝	
binding		6½ strips 2½" × 42"
Green Scraps	1	5 E patches, 22 leaves, 32 flower stems
vine		16 bias strips ¾" × 22"
Backing	3¾	2 panels 33" × 64"
Batting		64" × 64"

tips

For a simple lesson in paper-foundation piecing techniques, refer to Paper-Foundation Piecing on pages 108–109.

The rotary cutting diagrams for the G, Gr, and H patches require cutting a rectangle, marking the measurements as indicated, and aligning a ruler on the marks to trim to the correct shape.

Getting Started

Wash and press fabrics. Cut the patches and other pieces as listed in the materials and cutting box. Refer to pages 104–107 for Quilting Basics.

Making the Blocks

1 Trace or photocopy 24 of the Crown of Thorns arc pattern.

2 Foundation-piece the fabric units in numerical order. Make 24 arcs.

3 Join 1 A patch and 1 B patch to a Crown of Thorns arc, referring to Crown of Thorns Block Piecing.

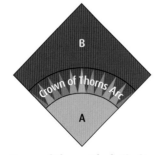

**Crown of Thorns Block Piecing
Make 16.**

4 Make 16 Crown of Thorns blocks.

5 Join 1 A patch and 1 C patch to a Crown of Thorns arc, referring to Crown of Thorns Side Block Piecing.

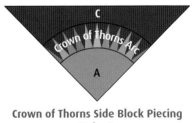

**Crown of Thorns Side Block Piecing
Make 8.**

6 Make 8 side blocks.

7 Remove the paper.

8 Trace or photocopy 5 of the Little Star pattern.

9 Cut the paper-foundation pattern along the marked line and cut away the center circle.

10 Foundation-piece the fabric units in numerical order.

11 To complete the circle, fold the stitched star with right sides of fabric together, aligning the cut edges of the paper foundation. Stitch along the cut edges.

12 Trim around the star, leaving a ¼" turn-under allowance.

13 Turn under edges and appliqué an E patch to the center of the Little Star.

14 Make 5 Little Stars.

15 Remove the paper.

16 The Little Stars are reverse appliquéd to a D patch to make a Little Star block. To make a circular frame for the star, cut a square of freezer paper that is at least 6½" × 6½". Fold the paper in half horizontally and vertically, and unfold. Use a drafting compass or a pencil on a string to draw a 5" circle in the center of the paper, on the non-shiny side, using the intersection of the horizontal and vertical folds as the center point.

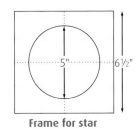

Frame for star

17 Cut away the circle on the drawn line and discard it. Place the freezer paper shiny side up on a pieced star, carefully centering the star in the cutout. If any of the points are covered by the paper, trim away the paper until the points just touch the edge of the circle.

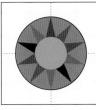

Center star in cutout.

18 Fold a D patch in half horizontally and vertically, lightly creasing the folds, and unfold. Iron the freezer paper, shiny side down, to the wrong side of the D patch, matching the creases.

19 Cut away the fabric ¼" inside the paper window.

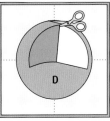

Cut ¼" inside window.

20 Clip into the turn-under allowance approximately every ½". Fold and press the turn-under allowance over the freezer paper in the center cutout.

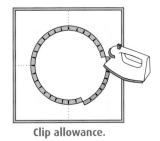

Clip allowance.

21 Center the star right-side up under the hole in the D patch, making sure that none of the points are hidden. Pin in place. Appliqué around the circle. Remove the paper. Trim the fabric to 6½" × 6½" square.

22 Make 5 Little Star blocks.

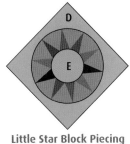

**Little Star Block Piecing
Make 5.**

23 Make a placement template for the appliqué by positioning and tracing the ½-pattern. Reposition the paper, match the dots, and trace the other half of the design. Use this template to arrange the appliqué on all of the F, G, Gr, and H patches, beginning at the square end of the patches and marking toward the angled end. Flip the pattern as needed to create the design, adjusting the placement of the flowers to fit the patch and referring to Quilt Assembly and Appliqué Placement.

24 To make the vines, fold the green strips in thirds, wrong sides together, and press.

25 Appliqué the stems first, and then the vines, flowers, and leaves.

Assembling the Quilt Top

1 Join 4 Crown of Thorns blocks into a block unit.

2 Make 4 block units.

3 Join the block units, side and star blocks, and F, G, Gr, and H patches in diagonal rows, referring to Quilt Assembly and Appliqué Placement.

4 Press the seam allowances away from the blocks.

5 Join the rows.

Quilting and Finishing

1 Mark the quilting motif in each A, B, and C patch, referring to Quilting Placement.

Quilt Assembly and Appliqué Placement

Quilting Placement

2 Layer and baste the quilt backing, batting, and top.

3 Quilt the motifs as marked. Quilt around the appliqué and along the block patches.

4 Trim quilt backing and batting even with the quilt top.

5 Join 2½"-wide strips diagonally to make the binding. Bind the quilt.

ROTARY CUTTING

Measurements include ¼" seam allowance.
Align arrows with lengthwise or crosswise grain of fabric.

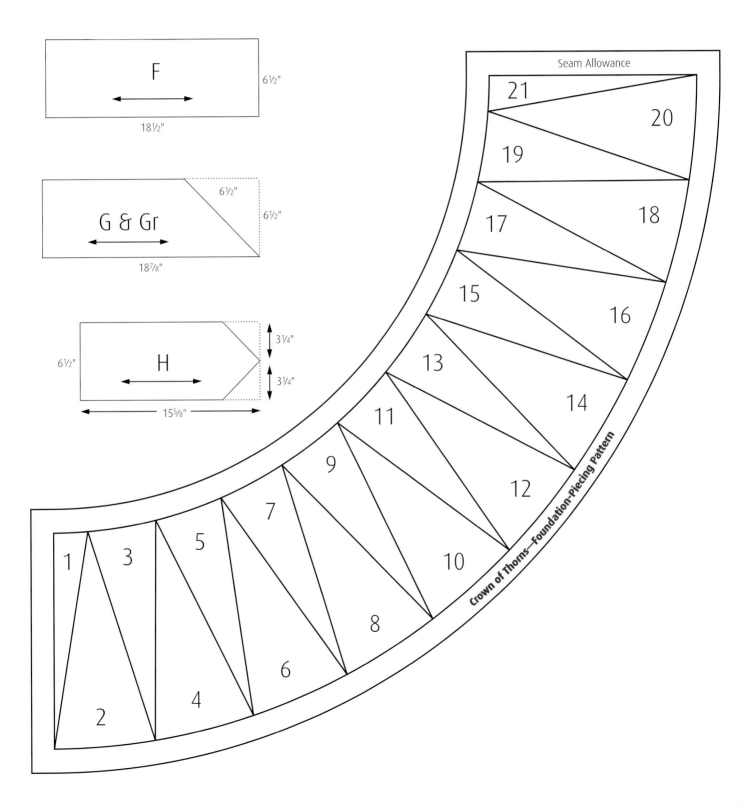

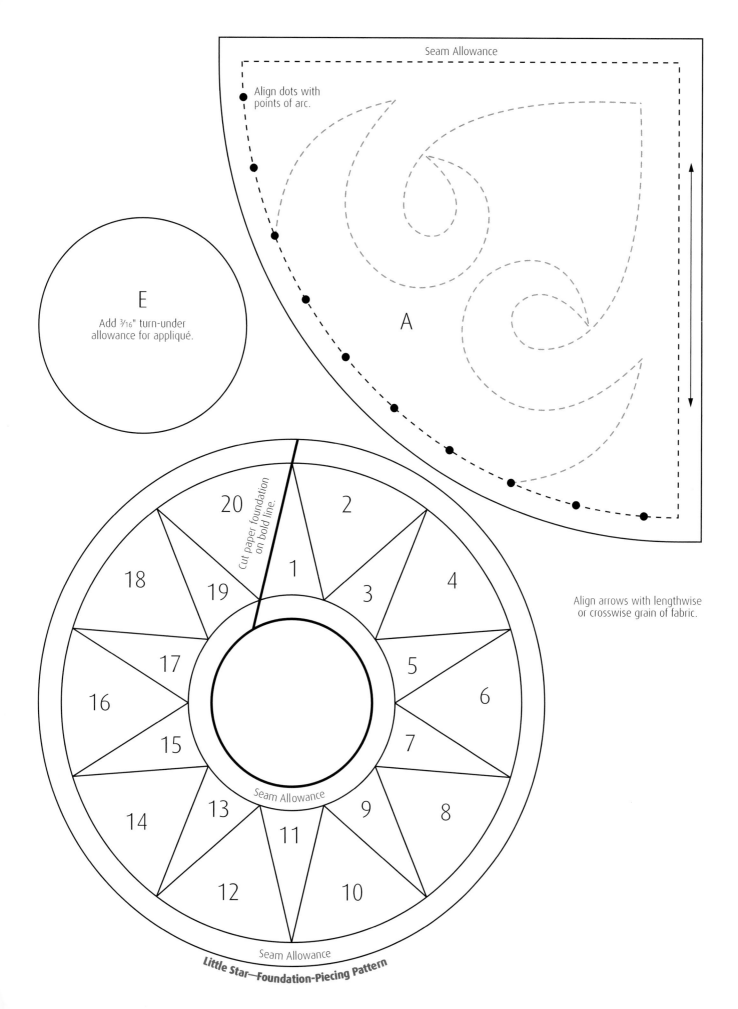

Seam Allowance

Align dots with
points of arc.

A

E

Add ³⁄₁₆" turn-under
allowance for appliqué.

cut paper foundation
on bold line.

20

2

1

18

19

3

4

17

5

16

6

15

7

Seam Allowance

14

13

9

8

11

12

10

Seam Allowance

Align arrows with lengthwise
or crosswise grain of fabric.

Little Star—Foundation-Piecing Pattern

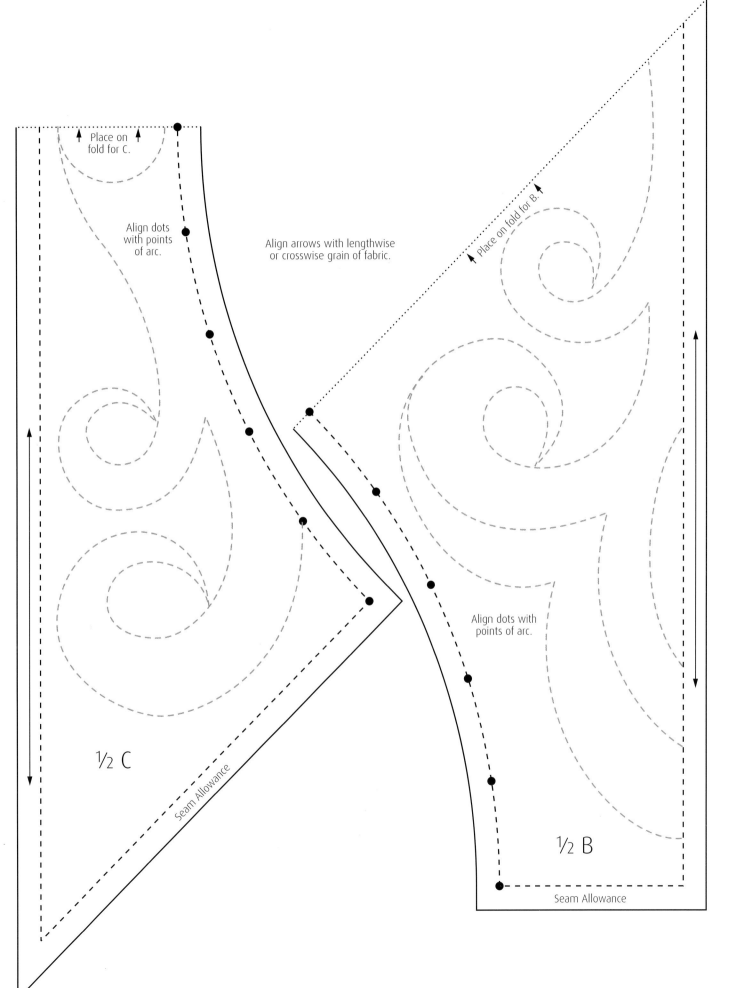

Place on fold for C.

Align dots with points of arc.

Align arrows with lengthwise or crosswise grain of fabric.

Place on fold for B.

Align dots with points of arc.

½ C

Seam Allowance

½ B

Seam Allowance

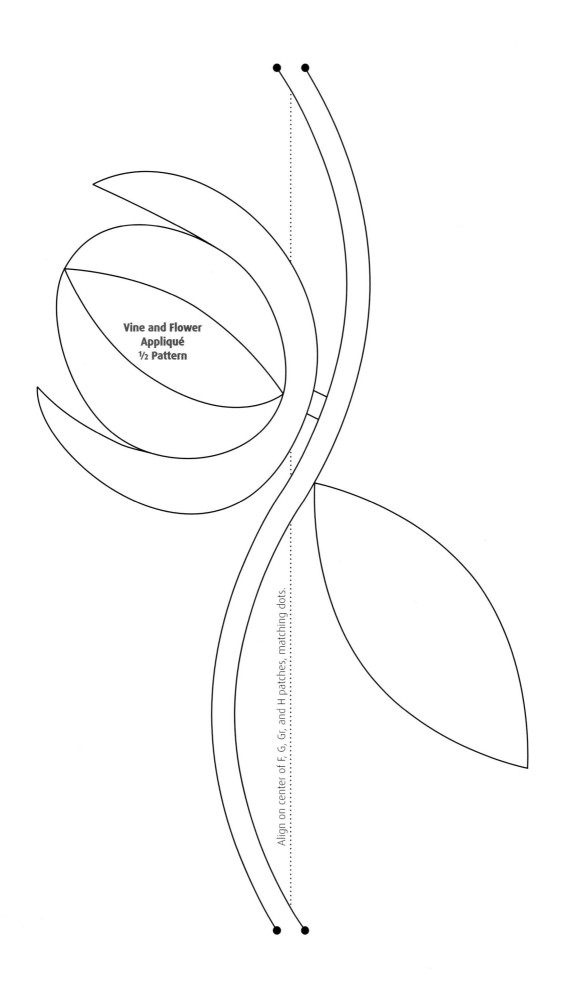

**Vine and Flower
Appliqué
½ Pattern**

Align on center of F, G, Gr, and H patches, matching dots.

A Gift Tied Up with Bows

PEGGY THURSTON AND GERRY SWEEM

*When Peggy Thurston of Reseda, California, drew the name of Gerry Sweem, also
of Reseda, in a Christmas exchange, she wanted to make something special.
Working on it for four years, she made a pieced top based on an antique quilt.
Gerry added the dogtooth and swag borders and then hand quilted it.*

Made by Peggy Thurston and Gerry Sweem. Quilted by Gerry Sweem.

Materials and Cutting

BLOCK SIZE: 3" × 3", 11" × 11"

QUILT SIZE: 79½" × 79½"

- ◆ Requirements are based on 42" fabric width.
- ◆ Borders include 2" extra length plus seam allowances. Measure your quilt and cut to size.
- ◆ Read all instructions before cutting.

MATERIALS	YARDS	CUTTING
Cream Print	2½	
borders		4 at 10" × 81¾"
White/Cream Scraps	3	96 C patches, 60 D patches, 24 F patches, 504 G patches,
		492 H patches
Medium/Dark Scraps	4½	1224 A patches, 288 B patches, 120 E patches, 1008 F patches,
		12 J patches
Green Print #1	1⅞ [*⅝]	144 I patches
inner borders		4 at 1" × 62¾"
Green Print #2	¾	20 swags
Red Print #1	½	20 bows
Red Print #2	2⅝ [*1½]	
dogtooth borders		4 at 3" × 80"
binding		4 strips 2½" × 84"
Backing	5	2 panels 42" × 84"
Batting		84" × 84"

* Yardage given in [ ] is for borders cut crosswise and pieced.

✸tips

While the blocks were created using scrap fabrics, the designer used red/yellow/red fabrics consistently in the centers of the Z blocks.

The 12 sash stars at the juncture of the sashes were pieced with yellow backgrounds.

Getting Started

Wash and press fabrics. Cut the patches and other pieces as listed in the materials and cutting box. Refer to pages 104–107 for Quilting Basics.

Making the Blocks

1 Join A, C, and D patches to make a Z block, referring to Block Z Piecing.

Block Z Piecing
Make 12.

2 Make 12 Z blocks.

3 Join A, C, and D patches to make half Z blocks, referring to Half Block Z Piecing.

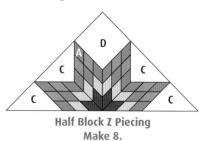

Half Block Z Piecing
Make 8.

4 Make 8 half Z blocks.

5 Join A and C patches to make quarter Z blocks, referring to Quarter Block Z Piecing.

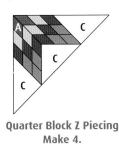

Quarter Block Z Piecing
Make 4.

6 Make 4 quarter Z blocks.

7 Join, B, C, and D patches to make a Y block, referring to Block Y Piecing.

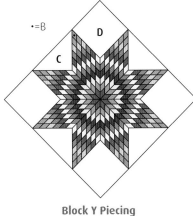

Block Y Piecing
Make 1.

8 Make 1 Y block.

9 Join E, F, G, and H patches to make sash stars, referring to Sash Star Piecing.

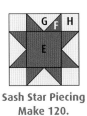

Sash Star Piecing
Make 120.

10 Make 120 sash stars.

11 Join F, G, H, and J patches to make half sash stars, referring to Half Sash Star Piecing.

Half Sash Star Piecing
Make 12.

12 Make 12 half sash stars.

13 Join 3 sash stars with 4 I patches to make a sash unit, referring to Sash Unit Piecing, beginning with an I patch and alternating I patches and sash stars.

14 Make 36 sash units.

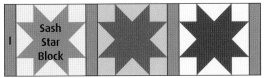

Sash Unit Piecing
Make 36.

Assembling the Quilt Top

1 Arrange the blocks and sashes in diagonal rows on a large, flat surface, referring to Partial Quilt Assembly for block positioning. The Y block is in the center of the quilt. The ends of the sash rows require a half sash star block, the ends of the block rows require a half Z block, and the corners require a quarter Z block.

2 Join the rows.

3 Fold a cream border in half and crease lightly to mark the center. Center a green swag at the center mark. Work out from the center, and arrange the swags and bows along the length of the cream border, saving the corner bows until the borders have been stitched to the quilt.

4 Appliqué the swags and bows to the border.

5 Repeat for the 3 remaining cream borders.

6 Appliqué the red sawtooth points along the outer edges of the borders using the following technique from Elly Sienkiewicz.

7 Find the center of a red dogtooth border strip and mark a dot ⅛" from the edge of the fabric at this point.

8 Measure along the strip in both directions, marking dots across the border at 1⅛" intervals. The last dot may be less than 1" from the end.

Center
Measure along the strip.

Partial Quilt Assembly

13 Continue as in Step 12 along the length of the strip, leaving the last 2 dogteeth unstitched.

14 Repeat for the 3 remaining red dogtooth border strips.

15 Match the center of an inner green border to the center of a cream border along the edge with the tops of the bows.

16 Join the borders to make a border unit.

17 Repeat for the 3 remaining borders.

18 Center a border unit at the top of the quilt. Join the border unit to the quilt top, starting and stopping stitching ¼" from the ends.

19 Repeat for the 3 remaining borders on the bottom and sides of the quilt top. Press the seam allowances toward the borders.

20 Turn the corner of the top border under at a 45° angle to preview the mitered corner. See how the dogtooth triangles meet in the corner. Make adjustments as needed and complete the stitching on the last dogtooth patches.

21 Miter the border corners, referring to Quilting Basics on pages 104–105.

22 Appliqué the corner bows to the cream border.

9 Align the center of a dogtooth strip with the center of a cream border.

10 Baste the dogtooth strip to the cream border, matching centers and keeping long, raw edges even.

11 Beginning with the center dot, make a 2"-long vertical cut into the dogtooth strip. Skip a dot, and make a similar cut at the third dot. Continue in this manner along the length of the strip. Do not cut along the last 3 dots at this time.

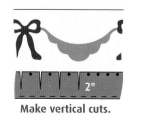

Make vertical cuts.

12 Fold the right side of a cut edge under and appliqué the fold to the cream border. Stop stitching at the last, uncut, marked dot. Do not break the thread. Turn under the other side of the point and appliqué it in place. The fabric folded beneath the point can be trimmed if needed. Turn under both sides of the next dogtooth and appliqué, taking 2 extra stitches at the inside V between the triangles.

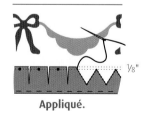

Appliqué.

Quilting and Finishing

1 Mark the quilting motif in each D patch and half the motif in each C patch, referring to Quilting Placement. Mark diagonal lines ½" apart in the cream border, not marking over the appliqué.

2 Layer and baste the quilt backing, batting, and top.

3 Quilt in-the-ditch around the patches in the large blocks. Quilt diagonal, horizontal, and vertical lines through the sash stars. Quilt down the middle of the I patches, around the appliqué, and on the marked lines and motifs.

4 Trim quilt backing and batting even with the quilt top.

5 Join 2½"-wide strips diagonally to make the binding. Bind the quilt.

Quilting Placement

ROTARY CUTTING

Measurements include ¼" seam allowance. Align arrows with lengthwise or crosswise grain of fabric.

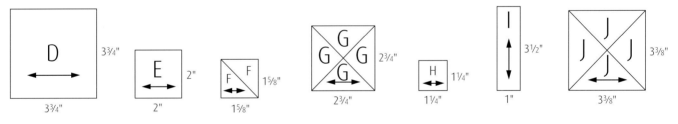

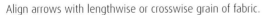
Align arrows with lengthwise or crosswise grain of fabric.

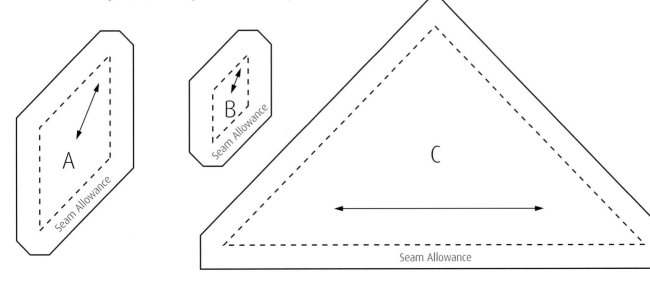

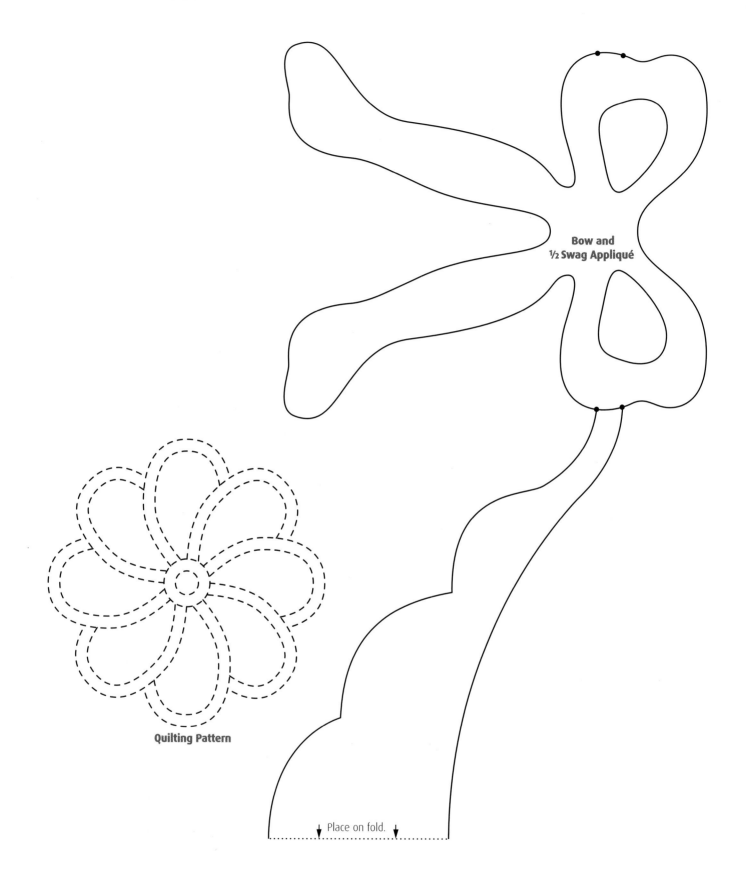

**Bow and
½ Swag Appliqué**

Quilting Pattern

↓ Place on fold. ↓

Working Out the Blues

RUTH HANS

Working out the Blues *was inspired by the quilt* Transformations *by Barbara Friedman and Lorane Feinberg, that appeared in Joen Wolfrom's book* The Visual Dance. *The pattern is based on the traditional North Wind block, also known as Corn and Beans at the turn of the twentieth century. The design looks difficult, but the quilt is actually made with different colorations of one simple-to-piece block set in diagonal rows. A multitude of overall curvy lines are quilted in the large patches and clamshell-like motifs in the small B patches. Both quilting designs add texture and interest.*

Made by Ruth Hans.

Materials and Cutting

BLOCK SIZE: 4½" × 4½"

QUILT SIZE: 81" × 81"

◆ Requirements are based on 42" fabric width.

◆ Borders include 2" extra length plus seam allowances. Measure your top and cut to size.

◆ Read all instructions before cutting.

MATERIALS	YARDS	CUTTING
Dark Blue Print	4	
borders		4 at 6" × 83½"
binding		4 strips 2½" × 85"
		76 A patches, 380 B patches, 44 D patches
Light Blue Water Print	2½	92 A patches, 460 B patches, 32 C patches
Light Scraps	2	96 A patches, 480 B patches
Medium Scraps	2¼	112 A patches, 560 B patches
Backing	5	2 panels 42" × 85"
Batting		85" × 85"

⭐ *tips* Following the block color-ings in the Quilt Assembly results in a visual pieced border around the center. One of the secrets of this design's success is the use of the same watery print where indicated. This blurs the edges of the blocks so that the eye is fooled into seeing the overall design instead of the individual blocks.

Each X, Y, and Z block requires 1 A patch and 5 B patches from one fabric, plus 1 A patch and 5 B patches from a second fabric. When making the blocks, keep the blocks separated by type.

For patches A, B, and D you can ei-ther rotary cut the squares, then cut them as needed, or you can make templates. Both are given on page 84.

Getting Started

Wash and press fabrics. Cut the patches and other pieces as listed in the materials and cutting box. Refer to pages 104–107 for Quilting Basics.

Making the Blocks

1 Join A and B patches to make an X block from the dark blue print and the light blue water print, referring to Block X Piecing.

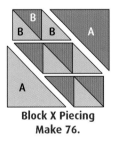

Block X Piecing
Make 76.

2 Make 76 X blocks.

3 Join A and B patches to make a Y block from the light blue water print and the medium scraps, referring to Block Y Piecing.

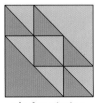

Block Y Piecing
Make 16.

4 Make 16 Y blocks.

5 Join A and B patches to make a Z block from the medium scraps and the light scraps, referring to Block Z Piecing.

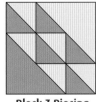

Block Z Piecing
Make 96.

6 Make 96 Z blocks.

Assembling the Quilt Top

1 Arrange the blocks, C patches, and D patches in diagonal rows on a large, flat surface, referring to Quilt Assembly Without Outer Border for block positioning. Note that each block is turned in a specific direction so that the blocks in the center of the

quilt form dark squares where the medium A patches meet, and the outer blocks form the pieced border.

2 Join the rows.

3 Sew the borders to the sides of the quilt, referring to the mitered corner borders section of Quilting Basics on pages 104–105. Sew the borders to the top and bottom. Press the seam allowances toward the borders.

4 Miter the corners.

Quilting and Finishing

1 Mark the Sea Grass quilting motifs in each A and D patch, referring to Quilting Placement. Mark 2 large motifs in each C square. Mark the curve in each B patch, connecting the lines as shown. If quilting the Sea Grass motifs in the outer border, mark a large motif ¼" away from the seam of each D patch, making the motifs meet at the mitered corners as shown.

2 Layer and baste the quilt backing, batting, and top.

3 Quilt the curves and motifs as marked.

4 Trim quilt backing and batting even with the quilt top.

5 Join 2½"-wide strips diagonally to make the binding. Bind the quilt.

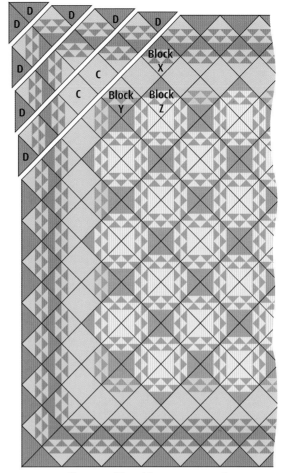

Quilt Assembly Without Outer Border

Quilting Placement

ROTARY CUTTING
Measurements include ¼" seam allowance. Align arrows with lengthwise or crosswise grain of fabric.

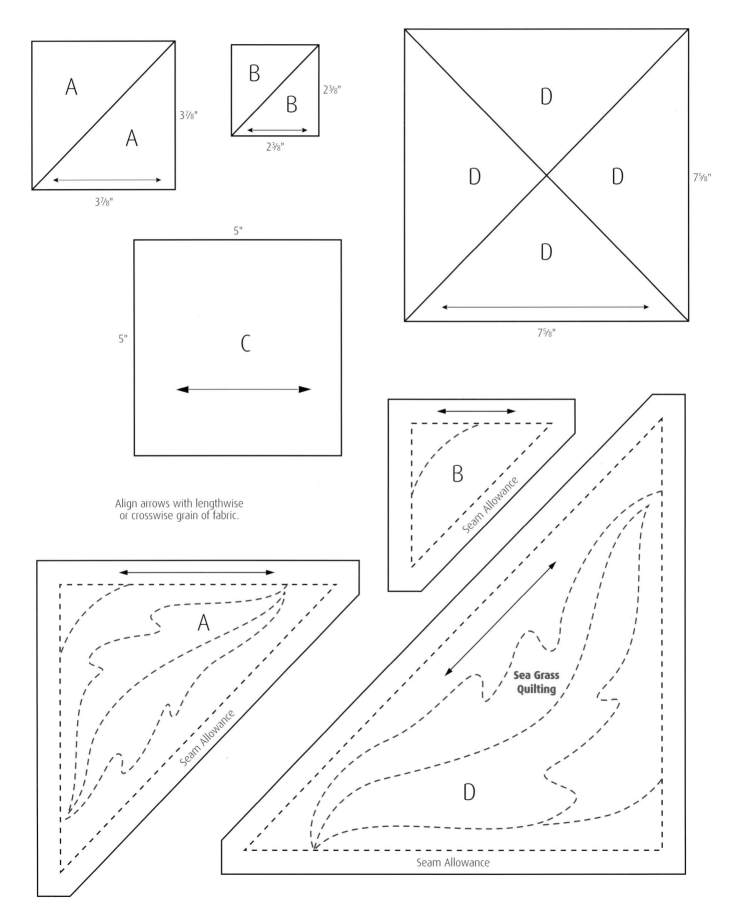

Align arrows with lengthwise
or crosswise grain of fabric.

Sea Grass
Quilting

Traveling Stars with Sunbursts

KATHLEEN McCRADY

Kathleen McCrady, of Austin, Texas, has been a quiltmaker since she was a teenager when she learned to quilt with her mother. Traveling Stars with Sunbursts is one of her most recent quilts. She hand pieced the stars and sunbursts over a period of several years, while traveling to various quilt events and on family visits. She notes the nine-block set was easy, but it took her a long time to decide on a border; drafting the half-sunbursts to fit the border became a challenge, and took much longer to piece than the stars.

Made by Kathleen McCrady.

Materials and Cutting

BLOCK SIZE: 18" × 18"

QUILT SIZE: 69¼" × 69¼"

- ◆ Requirements are based on 42" fabric width.
- ◆ Pieced borders are the exact length required plus seam allowances.
- ◆ Strip borders include 2" extra length plus seam allowance. Measure your top and cut to size.
- ◆ Read all instructions before cutting.

MATERIALS	YARDS	CUTTING
Background Print	*3	12 B patches, 16 C patches, 8 D patches, 4 E patches,
		20 G patches, 20 Gr patches, 20 H patches, 20 Hr patches,
		20 I patches, 20 Ir patches, 20 J patches, 20 Jr patches,
		16 K patches, 16 L patches, 16 M patches, 16 N patches,
		16 O patches, 4 P patches
Dark Brown Print	1¾	
borders		4 at 1½" × 58½"
binding		5 strips 2½" × 59"
		144 A patches
Gold Print Scraps	⅞	216 A patches
Tan Print Scraps	*1¼	72 A patches, 216 F patches
Red Print Scraps	*1½	216 A patches, 232 F patches
Brown Print Scraps	*½	128 F patches
Stripe Print Scraps	*½	144 F patches
Backing	4⅜	2 panels 37" × 74"
Batting		74" × 74"

* More yardage is required for fussy-cutting patches.

tips

The A and F patches can be cut with the grain of the fabric along one side or through the center, depending on the desired effect of the print in the block. The quilt-maker fussy-cut the fabrics so that some prints twirl around the star and others radiate from the center.

The background patches are cut so that the directional print is upright in the body of the quilt. The quiltmaker cut the C patches that are on point with the grainline on the diagonal of the square. This allows the print to remain in the correct orientation. Likewise, half the B and D patches were cut on the crosswise grain, and the other half were cut lengthwise.

The red and brown sunbursts are alternated around the quilt.

Getting Started

Wash and press fabrics. Cut the patches and other pieces as listed in the materials and cutting box. Refer to pages 104–107 for Quilting Basics.

Making the Blocks

1 Join 72 A patches to make a pieced star, referring to Star Piecing. Stop stitching at the outer-edge seamline of the stars to allow for set-ins.

2 Make 9 pieced stars.

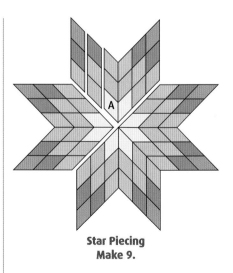

**Star Piecing
Make 9.**

Assembling the Quilt Top

1 Join pieced stars with B, C, D, and E patches, referring to Partial Quilt Assembly and being careful to piece the background patches in the correct position so that the print will remain upright.

2 Sew the borders to the sides of the quilt, referring to the mitered corner borders section of Quilting Basics on pages 104–105. Sew the borders to the top and bottom. Press the seam allowances toward the borders.

3 Miter the corners.

4 Join F patches with background patches G–P to make units, referring to Partial Quilt Assembly and sewing just to the seamlines to allow for set-ins.

5 Join the units to make sunburst borders, referring to the quilt photo on page 85 for color placement.

6 Make 2 short side borders and 2 long top and bottom borders.

7 Sew the side borders to the sides of the quilt. Sew the borders to the top and bottom of the quilt. Press the seam allowances toward the borders.

Quilting and Finishing

1 Layer and baste the quilt backing, batting, and top.

2 Quilt in-the-ditch around the star and sunburst patches. Quilt along the print in the background patches.

3 Trim quilt backing and batting even with the quilt top.

4 Join 2½"-wide strips diagonally to make the binding. Bind the quilt.

Partial Quilt Assembly

ROTARY CUTTING
Measurements include ¼" seam allowance. Align arrows with lengthwise or crosswise grain of fabric.

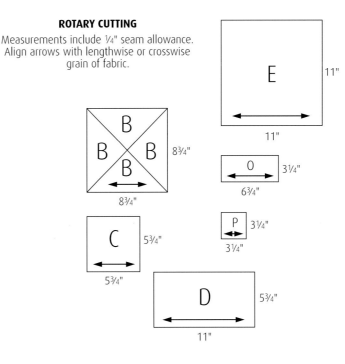

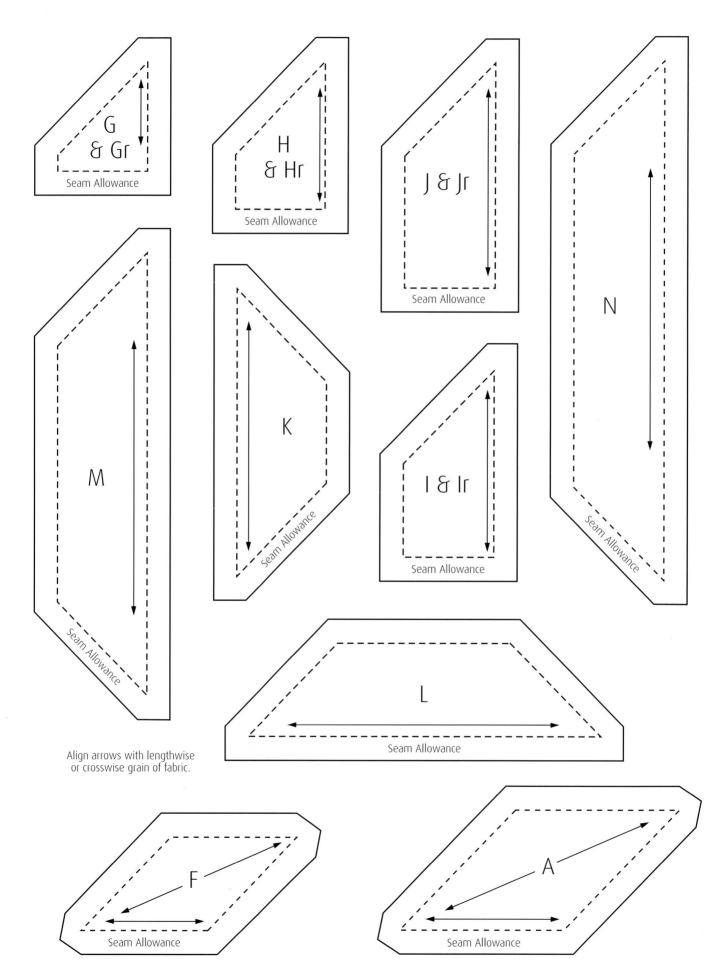

G
& Gr
Seam Allowance

H
& Hr
Seam Allowance

J & Jr
Seam Allowance

N
Seam Allowance

M
Seam Allowance

K
Seam Allowance

I & Ir
Seam Allowance

L
Seam Allowance

Align arrows with lengthwise
or crosswise grain of fabric.

F
Seam Allowance

A
Seam Allowance

Hot Tropical Sundae

JILL BEZENCON

Using more than fifty different fabrics from her stash, along with some hand-dyes, Jill Bezencon of Whangaparaoa, New Zealand, set out to reinterpret a traditional pattern with nontraditional fabrics in Hot Tropical Sundae. She used specialty threads for the big-stitch quilting, and various stitches, buttons, and thread ties as embellishments.

Made by Jill Bezencon.

Materials and Cutting

QUILT SIZE: 70" × 70"

◆ Requirements are based on 42" fabric width.

◆ Borders are the exact length required plus seam allowances.

◆ Read all instructions before cutting.

MATERIALS	YARDS	CUTTING
Orange/Red Print	1⅝	58 D patches, 16 E patches
Dark Brown Print	⅝	16 D patches, 10 E patches
Green Print	⅓	10 D patches, 2 E patches
Black/Brown Dot	1⅞ [*½]	
inner borders (sides)		2 at 2½" × 60½"
inner borders (top/bottom)		2 at 2½" × 56½"
Black Print	2⅛ [*⅝]	
outer borders (sides)		2 at 2½" × 70½"
outer borders (top/bottom)		2 at 2½" × 66½"
Bright and Dark Scraps	4	49 A patches, 196 B patches, 196 C patches, 84 F patches, 168 G patches
Dark Multicolor Print	⅝	
binding		7½ strips 2½" × 42"
Backing	4⅜	2 panels 38" × 74"
Batting		74" × 74"

*Yardage given in [ ] is for pieced borders cut crosswise and pieced.

Supplies: Buttons and specialty threads

tips Hand piecing the curved patches is recommended unless you are experienced with machine piecing curves. Make templates for A–E patches without seam allowances. Mark around the templates on the wrong side of the fabrics, including the dots. When cutting the patches, add a ¼" seam allowance by sight. If machine piecing, add ¼" to the templates.

For ease of construction, the pieced border has been slightly altered from the border shown in the quilt photo on page 89.

Getting Started

Wash and press fabrics. Cut the patches and other pieces as listed in the materials and cutting box. Refer to pages 104–107 for Quilting Basics.

Making the Blocks

1 Join A, B, and C patches to make a Nine-Patch unit, referring to Nine-Patch Unit.

**Nine-Patch Unit
Make 49.**

2 Make 49 Nine-Patch units.

3 Join F and G patches to make a corner unit, referring to Corner Unit.

**Corner Unit
Make 4.**

4 Make 4 corner units.

5 Join F and G patches to make a border unit, referring to Border Unit.

**Border Unit
Make 80.**

6 Make 80 border units.

Assembling the Quilt Top

1 Arrange the Nine-Patch units, D patches, and E patches in vertical rows, referring to Quilt Assembly and noting color placement of the D and E patches. The designer placed 4 orange D patches to create a flower in the lower left corner of the quilt top.

2 Pin a D patch to a Nine-Patch unit, aligning the dot on the D patch with the dot on the B patch. Align patches at beginning of curved seam, matching the seamlines, and pin.

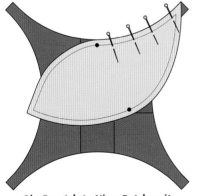

Pin D patch to Nine-Patch unit.

3 Sew along the seamline with small running stitches, checking the back often to be sure the seamlines remain aligned while stitching. Stop sewing at the center of the seam.

4 Align patches at the end of the curved seam and pin.

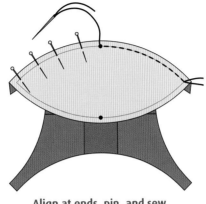

Align at ends, pin, and sew.

5 Sew to the end of the curved seam.

6 Join Nine-Patch units with D and E patches, referring to Quilt Assembly.

7 Sew the inner borders to the top and bottom of the quilt. Sew the inner borders to the sides. Press the seam allowances toward the borders.

8 Join 20 border units, referring to Quilt Assembly. Sew a corner unit to one end to complete the border.

9 Make 4 borders.

10 Sew the pieced borders to the top and bottom of the quilt, referring to the mitered corner borders section of Quilting Basics on pages 104–107. Sew pieced borders to the sides of the quilt. Press the seam allowances toward the borders.

11 Miter the corners.

12 Sew the outer borders to the top and bottom of the quilt. Sew the outer borders to the sides. Press the seam allowances toward the borders.

Quilting and Finishing

1 Mark the quilting motifs given on the D and E patches, as well as any other quilting motifs desired, referring to the quilt photo on page 89 for inspiration. The designer quilted free-form motifs and used heavy, contrasting thread to quilt some of them.

2 Layer and baste the quilt backing, batting, and top.

3 Quilt the motifs as marked.

4 Trim quilt backing and batting even with the quilt top.

5 Join 2½"-wide strips diagonally to make the binding. Bind the quilt.

Quilt Assembly

ROTARY CUTTING
Measurements include ¼" seam allowance.
Align arrows with lengthwise or crosswise grain of fabric.

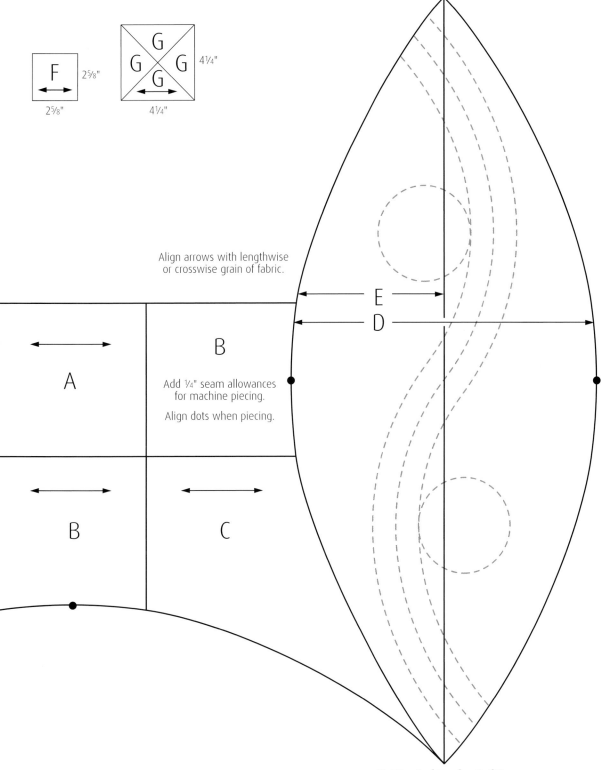

F
2⅝"
2⅝"

G G G G
4¼"
4¼"

Align arrows with lengthwise
or crosswise grain of fabric.

E
D

A

B

Add ¼" seam allowances
for machine piecing.

Align dots when piecing.

B

C

Hot Tropical Sundae Quilting

Twinkling Lone Star

CYNTHIA MICHAELS

Cynthia Michaels of Studio City, California, is an expert at making new fabric constructions look like vintage. She is a costume designer by profession, and sews period clothing for the opera and theater. Using those same skills, Cynthia made Twinkling Lone Star to look like an antique, choosing fabrics with a vintage "feel" and even overdyeing some fabrics to contribute to the appearance. Arrangements for the hand quilting were made by Miller's Dry Goods in Millersburg, Ohio.

Made by Cynthia Michaels. Quilter unknown.

Materials and Cutting

QUILT SIZE: 76" × 76"

◆ Requirements are based on 42" fabric width.

◆ Borders include 2" extra length plus seam allowances. Measure your top and cut to size.

◆ Read all instructions before cutting.

MATERIALS	YARDS	CUTTING
Assorted Print Scraps	5	512 A patches, 768 B patches
Light Tan Print	5/8	96 C patches, 96 D patches
Medium Tan Print	3/4	128 C patches, 128 D patches
Dark Tan Print	1 3/8	144 C patches, 192 D patches
inner borders*		4 at 2" × 72½"
Red Print	½	
middle borders*		4 at 2" × 75½"
Black Print	½	
outer borders*		4 at 1¾" × 78½"
Binding	5/8	8 strips 2½" × 42"
Backing	4¾	2 panels 41" × 80"
Batting		80" × 80"

* Borders are cut crosswise and pieced.

tips

The maker cut the A patches in each row of the diamond units from the same fabric. Though the fabrics are different in each unit, the values are similar. To achieve the look of dark or light circles around the star, place dark or light patches in the same place in each diamond unit.

Choose 2 different fabrics for the B patches in each small star block. All of the tan background fabrics are the same print. Cynthia overdyed the fabric to create the medium and dark tans. For those who prefer not to overdye, 3 different fabrics can be purchased to achieve the 3 values.

Set-in seams are required to construct the small star and half-star blocks and to set the quilt top together. The seam allowances on the set-ins must be left unstitched. To mark the start and stop points for stitching, put dots on the wrong side of the appropriate patches where the seamline begins and ends. Match these points when aligning the units, pin, and stitch only between the dots.

Getting Started

Wash and press fabrics. Cut the patches and other pieces as listed in the materials and cutting box. Refer to pages 104–107 for Quilting Basics.

Making the Blocks

1 Join the A patches in 8 rows of 8 patches each, referring to Diamond Unit Piecing.

Diamond Unit Piecing
Make 8.

2 Join the rows.

3 Make 8 diamond units.

4 Join 4 diamond units together to make half of the star, referring to Quilt Assembly on the next page, marking the dots, and leaving the seam allowances for the set-ins unstitched. Repeat for the remaining 4 diamond units.

5 Sew the star halves together.

6 Press the seam allowances in the same direction, making a swirl that reduces the bulk, as shown in Center Pressing.

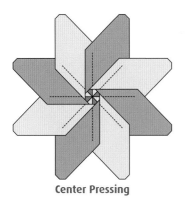

Center Pressing

7 Join B, C, and D patches to make a small star block, referring to Small Star Block Piecing, and marking dots as needed on the patches.

**Small Star Block Piecing
Make 88.**

8 Make 88 small star blocks.

9 Join 4 small star blocks to make a row.

10 Make 4 rows.

11 Join the rows to make a corner square.

12 Make 4 corner squares.

13 Join B, C, and D patches to make a half-star block, referring to Half-Star Block Piecing, and marking dots as needed on the patches.

**Half-Star Block Piecing
Make 16.**

14 Make 16 half-star blocks.

15 Join 6 star blocks with 4 half-star blocks to make a side triangle, referring to Side Triangle Piecing.

16 Make 4 side triangles.

Assembling the Quilt Top

1 Join a corner square to the Lone Star by aligning one edge of the square with one side of a diamond unit and pinning in place. Refer to Quilt Assembly for placement. Begin sewing at the inside corner. The corner unit is longer than the edge of the diamond unit, so there will be extra length extending beyond the point. This extra length creates a floating star effect in which the points do not extend to the edge of the background. Add all 4 corner squares to the star.

2 Join a side triangle to the Lone Star by aligning the edge of the triangle with the other side of the diamond unit and pinning in place. Refer to Quilt Assembly for placement. Begin sewing at the inside corner. The side triangle will continue over the corner of the corner square.

3 Repeat for the remaining side triangles.

**Side Triangle Piecing
Make 4.**

Center

Border Unit

Quilt Assembly

4 Press the seam allowances open.

5 Trim the excess fabric on the corner squares, where they meet the side triangles, leaving a ¼" seam allowance.

6 Match the centers of an inner, a middle, and an outer border. Join the borders. Repeat for the remaining borders.

7 Sew assembled borders to the sides of the quilt, starting and stopping stitching ¼" from each edge. Sew the borders to the top and bottom of the quilt.

8 Miter the corners, referring to Quilting Basics on pages 104–105.

Quilting and Finishing

1 Layer and baste the quilt backing, batting, and top.

2 Quilt as desired. The maker quilted a Baptist Fan design across the surface of the quilt.

3 Trim quilt backing and batting even with the quilt top.

4 Join 2½"-wide strips diagonally to make the binding. Bind the quilt.

Align arrows with lengthwise or crosswise grain of fabric.

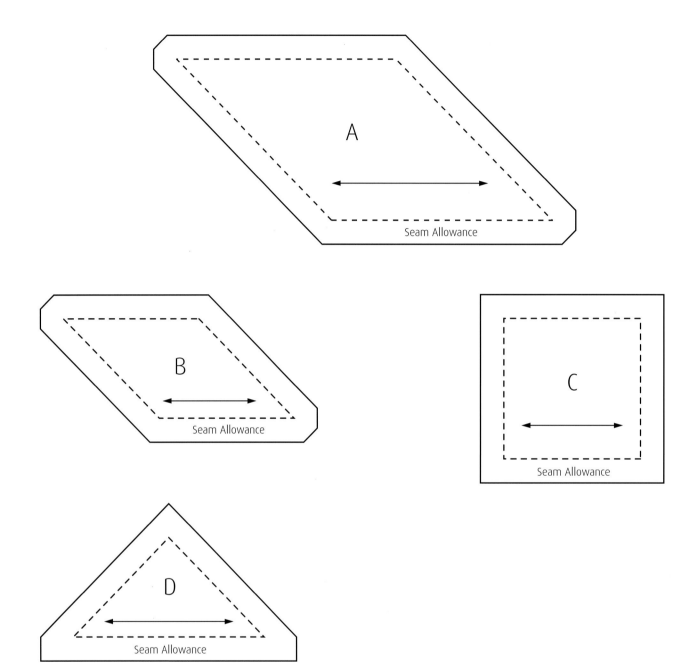

Snow Birds

JANINE HOLZMAN

Quiltmaker Janine Holzman designed this appliqué border as take-along handwork for travel. Going back and forth between her summer home in Alaska and her winter place in Arizona, Janine knew she would be spending time in airports. She always tried to have handwork ready to carry along. She used paper-foundation piecing methods to make the Pineapple blocks, and found it relaxing to make up a pile of blocks with blacks and browns contrasting with all sorts of bright scraps.

Made by Janine Holzman.

Materials and Cutting

BLOCK SIZE: 9" × 9"

QUILT SIZE: 78" × 78"

◆ Requirements are based on 42" fabric width.

◆ Pieced borders are the exact length required plus seam allowances.

◆ Strip borders include 2" extra length plus seam allowances. Measure your top and cut to size.

◆ Read all instructions before cutting.

MATERIALS	YARDS	CUTTING
Red Print	¾	
binding		8 strips 3" × 42"
Black Stripe	4½ [*2¼]	
middle borders		4 at 11" × 79"
Black/Brown Scraps	4	
inner borders		148 A patches
outer borders		204 A patches
foundation-piecing		144 each #2, 4, 6, 8, 10 patches
Light Scraps	5¼	bird patches
inner borders		144 A patches
outer borders		208 A patches
foundation-piecing		36 #1 patches; 144 each #3, 5, 7, 9, 11, 12 patches
Green Scraps	1	110 leaves
bias vine		1½" × 14 yards
Backing	4⅞	2 panels 42" × 82"
Batting		82" × 82"

* Amount of yardage needed if fabric is 44" wide.

tips

For the appliqué pieces, the quiltmaker added turn-under allowances and needle-turned the appliqué by hand. For certain parts of the motifs, such as the 3-color wings and the bird bodies, the quiltmaker first joined strips of fabric, then cut the appliqué motifs from the pieced fabric. For the 3-segment wing, sew a ⅞"-wide fabric strip between two wider strips and cut the wing from the pieced fabric.

For the A patch you can either rotary cut the squares, then cut them in quarters diagonally, or you can make a triangle template. Both are given on page 101.

Getting Started

Wash and press fabrics. Cut the patches and other pieces as listed in the materials and cutting box. Refer to pages 104–107 for Quilting Basics.

Making the Blocks

1 Enlarge the Pineapple Block Pattern 200% and trace or photocopy the block 36 times.

2 Use paper-foundation piecing methods to make the block. Sew the blocks in numerical order from 1–12, spiraling clockwise from the block center and referring to Pineapple Block pattern. Refer to pages 108–109 for paper-foundation piecing techniques.

3 Make 36 blocks.

4 Trim the blocks to 9½" × 9½".

Assembling the Quilt Top

1 Arrange the blocks in 6 rows of 6 blocks each.

2 Join 6 blocks into a row.

3 Make 6 rows.

4 Join the rows.

5 Remove the paper.

6 Join 36 light A patches with 37 black/brown A patches to make a pieced inner border.

7 Make 4 inner borders.

8 Sew inner borders to the sides, top, and bottom of the quilt top, stopping ¼" from the edge of the quilt top. Miter the corners.

9 Sew the middle borders to the sides, top, and bottom of the quilt top, stopping ¼" from the edge of the quilt top. Miter the corners. Trim the excess fabric.

10 Prepare the appliqué for 12 birds using your favorite method. Refer to Tips on page 100 for making 3-color wings.

11 To make the vines and branches, fold the green bias strips in thirds, wrong sides together, and press.

12 Position the vines and branches on the middle border and appliqué in place, referring to quilt photo on page 99 for placement.

13 Appliqué birds and leaves to the middle border as desired, referring to quilt photo on page 99 for placement and noting that the leaf placement is different on each border.

14 Join 52 light A patches with 51 black/brown A patches to make a pieced outer border.

15 Make 4 outer borders.

16 Sew outer borders to the sides, top, and bottom of the quilt top, stopping ¼" from the edge of the quilt top. Miter the corners.

17 Press seam allowances toward the middle border.

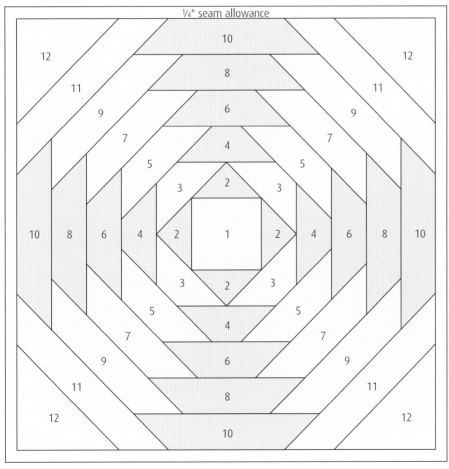

Pineapple Block—Foundation-Piecing Pattern
Enlarge 200%.

ROTARY CUTTING
Measurements include ¼" seam allowances.

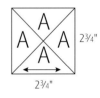

Align arrows with lengthwise or crosswise grain of fabric.

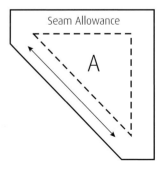

Quilting and Finishing

1 Layer and baste the quilt backing, batting, and top.

2 Quilt in-the-ditch around the appliqué. Quilt veins in the leaves and wing details on the birds. If desired, quilt diagonal lines across the quilt blocks in one direction and lines perpendicular to the quilt's edge in the middle border.

3 Trim quilt backing and batting ¼" beyond the edge of the quilt top.

4 Join 3"-wide strips diagonally to make a wider-than-usual binding. Bind the quilt, using a ¼" seam allowance and stitching ¼" from the edge of the quilt top (not the backing). Miter the corners, aligning the binding with the backing and batting (not the quilt top). Fold the binding to the back and stitch to the backing.

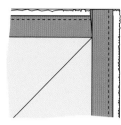

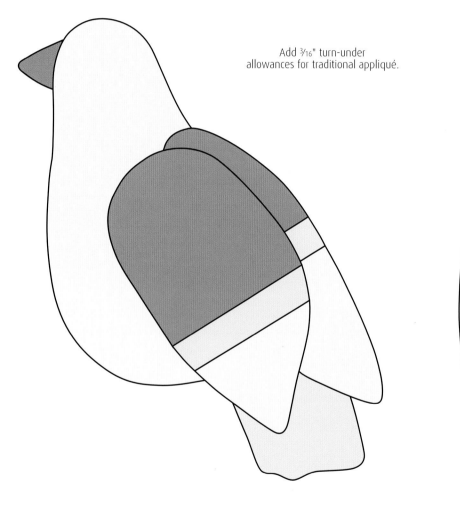

Add ³⁄₁₆" turn-under allowances for traditional appliqué.

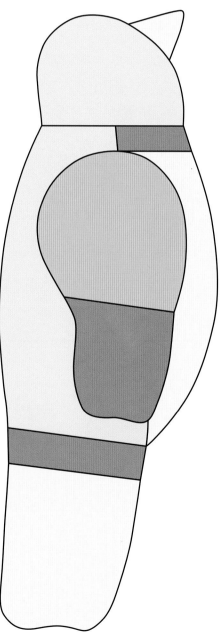

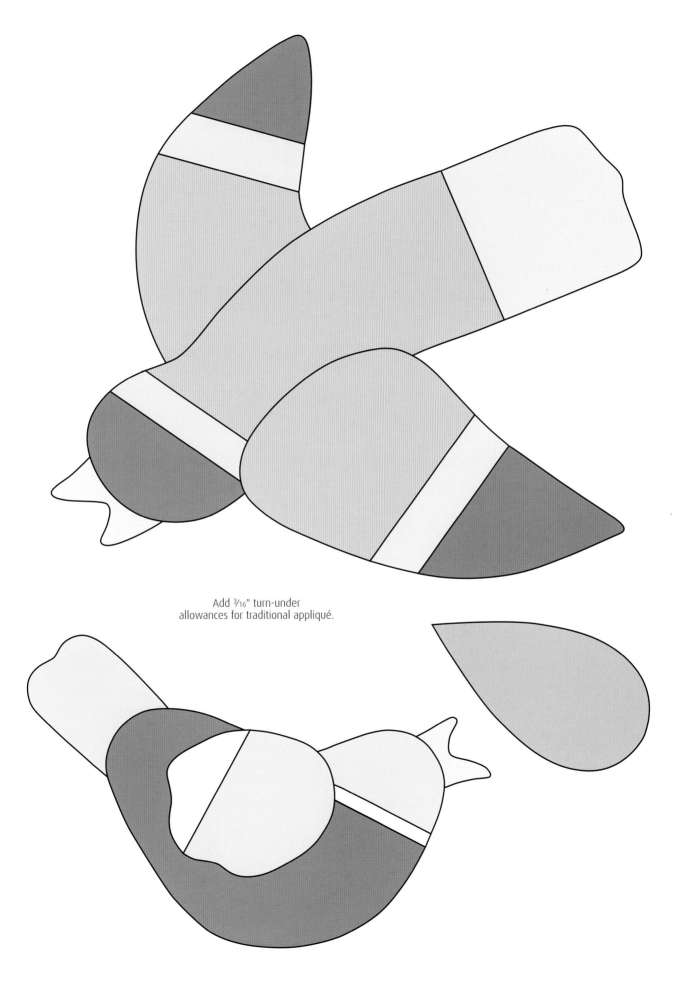

Add 3/16" turn-under
allowances for traditional appliqué.

Quilting Basics

Fabric requirements are based on a 42"-width; many fabrics shrink when washed, and widths vary by manufacturer. In cutting instructions, strips are generally cut on the crosswise grain.

General Guidelines

Seam Allowances

A ¼" seam allowance is used for most projects. It's a good idea to do a test seam before you begin sewing to check that your ¼" is accurate.

Pressing

In general, press seams toward the darker fabric. Press lightly in an up-and-down motion. Avoid using a very hot iron or over-ironing, which can distort shapes and blocks.

Borders

When border strips are to be cut on the crosswise grain, diagonally piece the strips together to achieve the needed lengths.

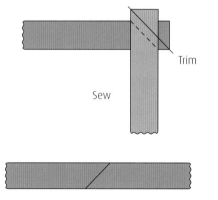

Butted Borders

In most cases the side borders are sewn on first. When you have finished the quilt top, measure it through the center vertically. This will be the length to cut the side borders. Place pins at the centers of all four sides of the quilt top, as well as in the center of each side border strip. Pin the side borders to the quilt top first, matching the center pins. Using a ¼" seam allowance, sew the borders to the quilt top and press.

Measure horizontally across the center of the quilt top including the side borders. This will be the length to cut the top and bottom borders. Repeat pinning, sewing, and pressing.

Mitered Corner Borders

Measure the length of the quilt top and add two times the width of your border, plus 2"–5". This is the length you need to cut or piece for the side borders .

Place pins at centers of both side borders and all four sides of the quilt top. From the center pin, measure in both directions, mark half of the measured length of the quilt top on both side borders. Pin, matching centers and the marked length of the side border to the edges of the quilt top. Stitch the strips to the sides of the quilt top. Stop and backstitch at the seam allowance line, ¼" in from the edge. The excess length will extend beyond each edge. Press seams toward border.

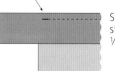

Start and stop stitching ¼" from edge.

Determine the length needed for the top and bottom border the same way, measuring the width of the quilt top through the center including each side border. Add 2"–5" to this measurement. Cut or piece these border strips. From the center of each border strip, in both directions, mark half of the measured width of the quilt top. Again, pin, stitch up to the ¼" seamline, and backstitch. The border strips extend beyond each end.

To create the miter, lay the corner on the ironing board. Working with the quilt right side up, lay one strip on top of the adjacent border.

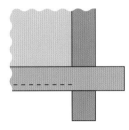

Fold the top border strip under itself so that it meets the edge of the outer border and forms a 45° angle. Press and pin the fold in place.

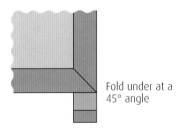

Fold under at a 45° angle

Position a 90° angle triangle or ruler over the corner to check that the corner is flat and square. When everything is in place press the fold firmly.

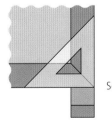

Square corner

Fold the top diagonally from the corner, right sides together, and align the long edges of the border strips. On the wrong side, place pins near the pressed fold in the corner to secure the border strips.

Beginning at the inside corner, backstitch and stitch along the fold toward the outside point, being careful not to allow any stretching to occur. Backstitch at the end. Trim the excess border fabric to ¼" seam allowance. Press the seam open.

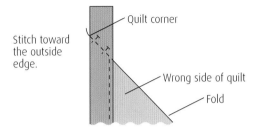

Stitch toward the outside edge.

Quilt corner

Wrong side of quilt

Fold

Backing

Plan on making the backing a minimum of 2" larger than the quilt top on all sides. Prewash the fabric, and trim the selvages before you piece.

To economize, you can piece the back from any leftover fabrics or blocks in your collection.

Batting

The type of batting to use is a personal decision; consult your local quilt shop. Cut batting approximately 2" larger on all sides than your quilt top.

Layering

Spread the backing wrong side up and tape the edges down with masking tape. (If you are working on carpet you can use T-pins to secure the backing to the carpet.) Center the batting on top, smoothing out any folds. Place the quilt top right side up on top of the batting and backing, making sure it's centered.

Basting

If you plan to machine quilt, pin baste the quilt layers together with safety pins placed a maximum of 3"–4" apart. Begin basting in the center and move toward the edges first in vertical, then horizontal, rows.

If you plan to hand quilt, baste the layers together with thread using a long needle and light-colored thread. Knot one end of the thread. Using stitches approximately the length of the needle, begin in the center and move out toward the edges.

Quilting

Quilting, whether by hand or machine, enhances the pieced or appliqué design of the quilt. You may choose to quilt in-the-ditch, echo the pieced or appliqué motifs, use patterns from quilting design books and stencils, or do your own free-motion quilting. Suggested quilting patterns are included in some of the projects.

Binding

Double Fold Straight Grain Binding (French Fold)

Trim excess batting and backing from the quilt. If you want a ¼" finished binding, cut the strips 2¼" wide and piece together with a diagonal seam to make a continuous binding strip. Press the seams open, then press the entire strip in half length-wise with wrong sides together. With raw edges even, pin the binding to the edge of the quilt a few inches away from the corner, and leave the first few inches of the binding unattached. Start sewing, using a ¼" seam allowance.

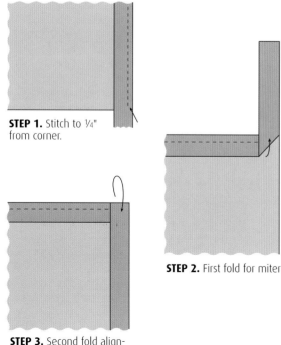

STEP 1. Stitch to ¼" from corner.

STEP 2. First fold for miter

STEP 3. Second fold alignment. Repeat in the same manner at all corners.

Stop ¼" away from the first corner (see Step 1), backstitch one stitch. Lift the presser foot and needle. Rotate the quilt one quarter turn. Fold the binding at a right angle so it extends straight above the quilt (see Step 2). Then bring the binding strip down even with the edge of the quilt (see Step 3). Begin sewing at the folded edge. Repeat for all 4 corners.

Continuous Bias Binding

A continuous bias involves using the same square sliced in half diagonally but sewing the triangles together so that you continuously cut the marked strips. The same instructions can be used to cut bias for piping. Cut the fabric for the bias binding or piping so it is a square. If yardage is ½ yard, cut an 18" square. Cut the square in half diagonally, creating two triangles.

Sew these triangles together as shown, using a ¼" seam allowance. Press the seam open.

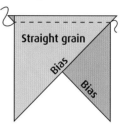

Using a ruler, mark the parallelogram with lines spaced the width you need to cut your bias. Cut along the first line about 5".

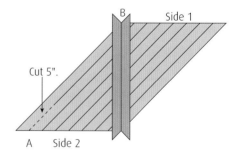

Join Side 1 and Side 2 to form a tube. Line A will line up with the raw edge at B. This will allow the first line to be offset by one strip width. Pin the raw ends together, right sides together, making sure that the lines match. Sew with a ¼" seam allowance. Press seams open.

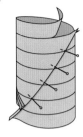

Finishing the Binding

This is one method of finishing the binding. Fold under the beginning end of the binding strip ¼". Lay the ending binding strip over the beginning folded end. Continue stitching the seam beyond the folded edge. Trim the excess binding. Fold the binding over the raw edges to the quilt back and hand stitch, mitering corners.

Machine Appliqué Using Fusible Adhesive

Lay the fusible web sheet paper-side up on the pattern and trace with a pencil. Trace detail lines with a permanent marker for ease in transferring to the fabric.

Use paper-cutting scissors to roughly cut out the pieces. Leave at least a ¼" border.

Following manufacturer's instructions, fuse the web patterns to the wrong side of the appliqué fabric. It helps to use an appliqué-pressing sheet to avoid getting the adhesive on your iron or ironing board.

Cut out the pieces along the pencil line. Do not remove the paper yet.

Transfer the detail lines to the fabric by placing the piece on a light table or up to the window and marking the fabric. Use pencil for this task—the lines will be covered by thread.

Remove the paper and position the appliqué piece on your project. Be sure the web (rough) side is down. Press in place, following the manufacturer's instructions.

Paper-Foundation Piecing

BY BARBARA FIEDLER

Foundation piecing is an accurate technique for sewing blocks that are difficult to piece. A little practice and knowing a few "do's and don'ts" will make you successful with this popular technique.

To help you understand this piecing method, study this foundation-pieced block and the illustrations of common foundation-piecing mistakes. For instruction, the correct stitching is shown in black and incorrect sewing is marked in red.

1 Trace or photocopy the complete foundation pattern, including all the numbers and lines. Without the block seam lines or cutting lines, you will not know where to sew or where to trim the block to its correct size.

2 Cut out the paper foundation beyond the outer line. The extra dimension is a good visual measure of size for those patches that lie along the block perimeter. If your patches extend beyond the foundation, you know they will be large enough.

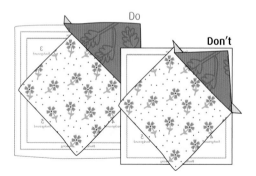

3 Always set your stitch length to a short setting, 18–20 stitches to the inch. ------------ Longer stitches won't

perforate the paper close enough so it will be harder to tear away the foundation and easier for the stitches to pull loose.

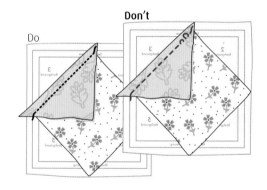

4 Check patch placement before you sew it to the foundation. If not, you could sew a patch with a seam allowance that is too narrow or miss sewing the patch to the foundation.

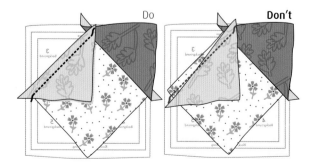

5 Stitch on the printed side of the foundation to easily follow the sewing line and sew exactly on the printed seam line. Sewing off the line will change the pattern or design.

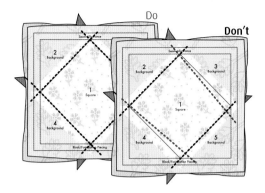

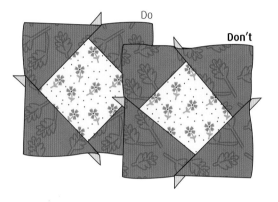

6 For every seam line, begin stitching ¼" before the seamline and continue ¼" beyond. If the stitching does not cross over the previous seamline, as consecutive patches are added a gap will exist in the patchwork. Backstitching does not take the place of cross seaming.

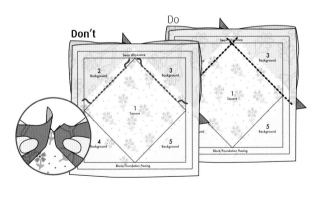

7 After each patch addition, trim the seam allowances to ¼". Narrower seam allowances can pull away from the stitching and leave a hole in the block.

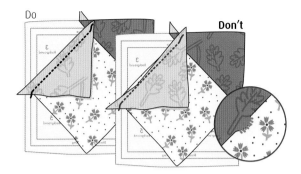

8 After a patch is added, open the patch from the fabric side and press the seam flat. Otherwise, you will have a tuck in the fabric and patches will not be the correct size.

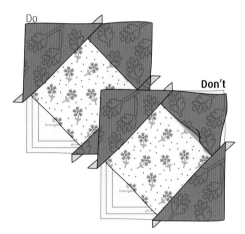

9 Trim the foundation precisely on the outside line after it is pieced. Careless cutting will give an inaccurate block size.

10 Leave the outer foundation lines unsewn. If you stitch the foundation perimeter, removing the paper will be difficult.

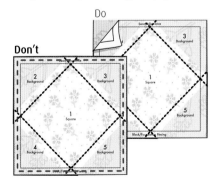

Note: Photocopying may cause distortion. Compare pattern copies to original for accuracy.

ABOUT THE AUTHOR

Mary Leman Austin has been part of *Quilter's Newsletter Magazine* since its inception in 1969. Her favorite part of the job has always been designing patterns for *QNM* readers, something she has less opportunity to do these days. Mary managed the art and production needs of the magazine until 1993, when she moved into editing. She was named *QNM's* Executive Director in 1996 when her mother Bonnie Leman retired.

She has judged quilt shows nationally and internationally, and is a member of the advisory council of the International Quilt Study Center. Her favorite quiltmaking technique is paper-foundation piecing.

OTHER FINE BOOKS FROM C&T PUBLISHING AND *QUILTER'S NEWSLETTER MAGAZINE*

Paper Piecing Picnic
From *Quilter's Newsletter Magazine* and *Quiltmaker*

You'll love these tried-and-true favorites. 16 fresh, fun, paper-pieced projects.

Paper Piecing Potpourri
From *Quilter's Newsletter Magazine*, *Quiltmaker*, and C&T Publishing

Quilter's Newsletter Magazine and *Quiltmaker* dish up another serving of 17 tried-and-true paper-pieced quilt designs.

All About Quilting from A to Z
From *Quilter's Newsletter Magazine*, *Quiltmaker*, and C&T Publishing

Everything you want to know about designing, creating, and living with quilts in one comprehensive volume! Famous quilt artists share their knowledge and expertise in six sections covering the basics and beyond.

FOR MORE INFORMATION

Ask for a free catalog:
C&T Publishing, Inc.
P.O. Box 1456
Lafayette, CA 94549
800-284-1114
email: ctinfo@ctpub.com
website: www.ctpub.com

QUILTING SUPPLIES

Cotton Patch Mail Order
3404 Hall Lane
Dept CTB
Lafayette, CA 94549
800-835-4418   925-283-7883
email: quiltusa@yahoo.com
website: www.quiltusa.com

Note: Fabrics used in the quilts shown may not be currently available because fabric manufacturers keep most fabrics in print for only a short time.

INDEX